1 $\frac{00}{Q}$

08-AHD-977

How to Beat JET LAG

A Practical Guide for Air Travelers

DAN A. OREN, M.D.

WALTER REICH, M.D.

NORMAN E. ROSENTHAL, M.D.

THOMAS A. WEHR, M.D.

Illustrations by Jeanette Kuvin Oren

A John Macrae Book
HENRY HOLT AND COMPANY
NEW YORK

For Our Wives and Children

Henry Holt and Company, Inc.
Publishers since 1866
115 West 18th Street
New York, New York 10011

Henry Holt® is a registered
trademark of Henry Holt and Company, Inc.

Library of Congress Cataloging-in-Publication Data

How to beat jet lag : a practical guide for air travelers / Dan A. Oren
. . . [et al.] ; illustrations by Jeanette Kuvin Oren. — 1st ed.
p. cm.
"A John Macrae book."
1. Jet lag. I. Oren, Dan A.
RC1076.J48J48 1993
613.6'8—dc20   93-17190
                                                CIP

ISBN 0-8050-2687-8 (An Owl Book: pbk)

Henry Holt books are available for special promotions and
premiums. For details contact: Director, Special Markets.

First Edition—1993

Designed by Claire Naylon Vaccaro

Printed in the United States of America
All first editions are printed on acid-free paper.∞

1   3   5   7   9   10   8   6   4   2

The authors are all senior psychiatrists and research scientists at the National
Institute of Mental Health. The views expressed in this book, and the
recommendations provided in it, are those of the authors; they are not those
of, nor are they endorsed by, the National Institute of Mental Health.

Contents

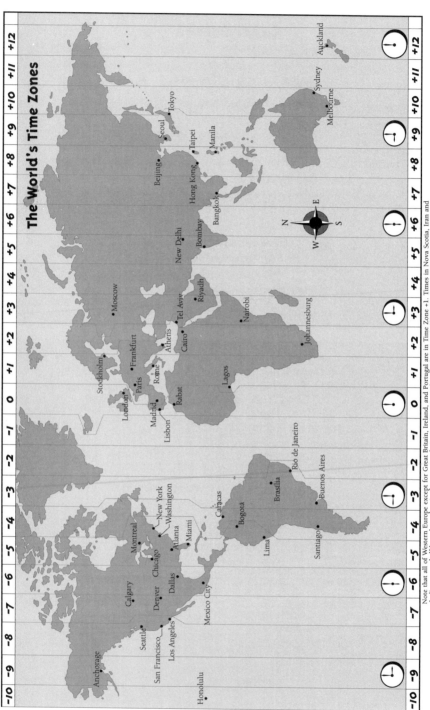

The World's Time Zones

Note that all of Western Europe except for Great Britain, Ireland, and Portugal are in Time Zone +1. Times in Nova Scotia, Iran and India are one-half hour later than in the zones to their west. Time in mid-Australia is one-half hour earlier than in the zone to its east.

The
SCIENCE and the TECHNIQUE

What Jet Lag Is
and How to Beat It

To seasoned travelers, jet lag is an irritatingly familiar experience. To the uninitiated, it may be an unpleasant surprise to experience the cluster of symptoms that typically afflicts travelers who fly east or west across a number of time zones. The symptoms of jet lag may last for several days and may disrupt your ability to concentrate, make decisions, or enjoy yourself. In this introductory section, we describe the common features of jet lag, explain their biological basis, and briefly summarize some exciting scientific findings that provide the key to overcoming this problem without the use of drugs. In recent years it has become apparent to scientists that exposure to light and to darkness plays a critical role in regulating the timing of our daily biological rhythms (also known as circadian rhythms). In later sections of this book, we will provide you with specific directions as to how you can use what has been learned in scientific research to manipulate light and darkness in specific ways so as to minimize your jet lag symptoms and enable you to function at your best when you travel across time zones.

The Symptoms of Jet Lag

Air travel can produce all sorts of discomforts, including muscle aches from sitting in a fixed position for prolonged periods, sinus trouble from changing air pressure in the cabin, and allergies from exposure to tobacco smoke. When we refer to jet lag, however, we are referring to a specific cluster of symptoms that are distinct from these other discomforts—symptoms that result from flying across time zones in either a westerly or an easterly direction. The most common symptoms of jet lag are feelings of drowsiness or lethargy, a tendency to fall asleep during the day or, conversely, the inability to fall asleep at night or a tendency to wake up too early in the morning. Jet lag may be associated with physical symptoms that result from having to stay awake when your body tells you it's bedtime.

Jet lag can also cause in difficulties in thinking and concentrating that may impair efficiency and judgment in ways that may be extremely costly to the business traveler and unpleasant for the vacationer. Imagine how effective you would be if someone woke you up at 4 o'clock in the morning and asked you to negotiate a major contract with representatives of a foreign corporation or conduct a meeting with important business associates. Think of how little you would be able to enjoy a scenic tour or a cocktail party in the early hours of the morning. Yet that is exactly how it may feel to the jet-lagged traveler. It may be 10:00 P.M. in New York, where you've just arrived, and an acceptable time for get-togethers and cocktails, However, in London it's 3:00 A.M., and your body is interested in nothing but sleep. When it's 4:00 P.M. in Tokyo, a perfectly reasonable time to be closing a business deal, it's 2:00 A.M. in Washington, D.C., the city from which you've just arrived for a meeting with Japanese business associates, and you may be too jet lagged to care, or even to know, whether you're talking in dollars or in yen. In summary, if your flight has just brought you across several time zones, the difference between the local time in the city of your arrival and your body's time, which is still set to match the time in the city from which you've just departed, has physical and psychological consequences that can be emotionally and even financially costly.

Long-distance plane travel is often associated with sleep loss, which also results in weariness and fatigue and can be mistaken for jet lag. It is important, however, to distinguish between these two different causes of daytime drowsiness because the symptoms of sleep deprivation can be managed successfully simply by catching up on lost sleep, whereas the symptoms of jet lag can be minimized by the more sophisticated approach outlined in the later chapters of this book. Jet lag occurs specifically after a flight across several time zones when the traveler's biological rhythms are out of sync with those of others living in the time zone of one's destination. These rhythms tend to be stable and do not shift rapidly to accommodate the rhythms of night and day in the new time zone. The steps outlined in this book will help shift them more rapidly and speed up the process of adaptation.

The severity of a person's jet lag depends on several factors. Most important of these is the number of time zones crossed during the flight. No jet lag results from flights between points north and south within the same time zone. Similarly, trips between cities just one time zone apart (for example, New York and Chicago) are unlikely to result in significant symptoms of jet lag. On trips between the West Coast of the United States and Western Europe, on the other hand, the traveler will cross nine time zones and severe symptoms of jet lag may result. In one study it took travelers who crossed this number of time zones an average of 12 days before they recovered completely from their jet lag.

A second factor is the direction of travel. Travelers flying eastward tend to have a harder time adjusting to the new time zone than those traveling westward. When you travel in an easterly direction, you will need to set your wristwatch ahead to a later time. Night will come sooner than in your time zone of origin and you will need to go to sleep earlier and wake up earlier than you would have needed to had you never taken the flight. For the first several days after arrival at your destination, however, your body rhythms will tend to make you want to go to sleep later and wake up later than those living in your new time zone. It is necessary to shift your rhythms earlier to bring them in sync with the new time zone—and the sooner the better. It is a more difficult task for most people to go to sleep earlier than usual than it is for them to stay up later than usual, which is necessary when one travels in a westerly direction.

The tendency to go to sleep later and wake up later than usual is often seen on weekends, when most people are less constrained by schedules than they are during the week. If you allow your rhythms to drift too much later during weekends, it can feel like a rude shock to have to wake up on time for work on Monday morning and shift your rhythms earlier, in line with the demands of a weekday schedule. The degree to which your body's sleep-wake rhythms are out of sync with local time following jet travel is often far more radical than this familiar weekly experience.

There appear to be internal factors related to an individual's own biological makeup that determine the ease or difficulty of adjusting to a new time zone. In other words, some people have much more difficulty with jet lag than others for reasons that are not well understood.

Until recently, very little was known about how to prevent, shorten, and overcome the symptoms of jet lag: one simply traveled and suffered. To be sure, nostrums such as eating or avoiding certain foods were recommended to help the traveler avert the discomfort of jet lag, but there was little or no scientific evidence to support these recommendations. During the past few years, scientific findings have led to an understanding of the basic processes that govern our normal biological rhythms and are disrupted, sometimes severely, when we fly across multiple time zones. These processes involve, to a large extent, our experience of the cycle of light and darkness that occurs during the 24-hour period of day and night. We have come to understand that light and darkness affect us quite specifically and powerfully. By influencing certain biological processes in our brain, light and darkness regulate, and usually stabilize, our biological rhythms. As a result of this new understanding, we can now recommend methods that can reset an air traveler's biological clock. These methods involve exposing the traveler to periods of light and dark at certain precise times during and after the flight so as to shift the traveler's biological clock into a rhythm that corresponds to the rhythm of persons living in the time zone of the traveler's destination.

If you are interested in understanding more about the principles on which this jet lag guide is based, read on. Such understanding is not necessary, however, for using this manual successfully; if you are less interested in the theory than in the nuts and bolts of how to minimize your own jet lag symptoms, simply skip some of the sections below and go directly to specific instructions for the trip you are taking. It would be helpful, however, to take a look at the section on page 14 titled, "Being in the Light and in the Dark," since it contains practical information that you will need in order to implement the guidelines in this manual.

Your Biological Rhythms

All living creatures, from single-celled organisms such as algae to human beings, show biological rhythms in their behavior and physiology. The most obvious behavioral rhythm in human beings is the daily pattern of sleeping and waking, but this is only one of a multitude of rhythmic and predictable behavior changes that occur over the course of each day. Other rhythmic processes include changes in body temperature, alertness, and the secretion of various hormones. Scientists working with many different species, including human beings, have shown that these daily rhythms are not merely a passive response to changes in the outside world but are generated by an internal body clock embedded in the brain.

The body's clock has a rhythm of its own. Even if you were to stay in a dark cave for many days without any access to the outside world and without knowledge of the time of day, the body clock would continue to dictate a pattern of sleeping and waking in a rhythm of slightly longer than 24 hours. It is this tendency for our intrinsic rhythms to exceed 24 hours in length that makes it easier for people to shift their rhythms later rather than earlier and to adjust to westward as opposed to eastward travel. If you were completely isolated from all external time cues, your biological rhythms would, over time, drift out of sync with the daily rhythms of the outside world. Under normal circumstances these rhythms run in sync with the 24-hour day-night cycle because environmental influences, especially light and darkness, reset the clock and keep them in harmony. It is these environmental influences that, over a number of days, bring the traveler's body clock in line with local time after a flight across several time zones. The object of this book is to help the traveler manipulate these environmental time cues rapidly, particularly during the flight and the first days after landing, so as to speed up the adjustment process and thereby avoid or minimize the symptoms of jet lag. This manipulation largely involves exposure to, or avoidance of, light at specific times during and after a particular flight.

Your biological clock tells you when it's time to go to sleep and wake up, when you need to rest and when you should be alert. When you travel across time zones, there's a time difference between your point of origin and your destination. In order to plan your activities in the new time zone, you typically adjust your watch earlier or later so that it corresponds to local time. In a very similar way, your body's clock needs to be reset earlier or later in its timing. But while your wristwatch can be adjusted within seconds, your body's clock may take days or even weeks to be adjusted to local time. Like a gyroscope, the body's clock has inertia and is not easily deflected from its habitual course. The symptoms of jet lag result from your circadian (daily) rhythms and body clock being temporarily out of sync with local time. To shorten the process of adjustment to local time we can take advantage of what we know about the influence of external time cues on our clock and their effects on our biological rhythms.

The Importance of Light and Dark

It is only relatively recently that we have become aware of the important influence of light and dark on the circadian rhythms of human beings. Several researchers have made important contributions to this understanding, including Drs. Alfred J. Lewy of the Oregon Health Sciences Center in Portland, David Minors and James Waterhouse of Manchester University in England, and Charles Czeisler and Richard Kronauer at Harvard University. These scientists extended the considerable body of research on circadian rhythms in animals to show that many, if not most, of the findings in other species apply to humans as well.

Dr. Lewy, Dr. Thomas Wehr, and their colleagues, working then at the National Institute of Mental Health, showed that bright light is capable of suppressing the secretion of the hormone melatonin. This hormone is secreted at night by the pineal gland, a pea-sized structure at the base of the brain. Although the functions of this hormone in human beings are not well understood, melatonin appears to have an influence on the timing of circadian rhythms. As such, it may ultimately have some value in the treatment of jet lag—and, in fact, has already been used for that purpose experimentally with some success. Melatonin is not currently available as a drug, so it cannot be used for treating jet lag in the general population.

The discovery that human melatonin secretion could be suppressed by environmental light was especially exciting since it implied that light was biologically active in humans (the influence of light and darkness on the circadian rhythms of animals had long been appreciated). Dr. Lewy and his colleagues suggested that light and darkness might influence circadian rhythms in human beings in the same way they do in other animals. They hypothesized that human beings would show a predictable relationship between the time of day when they are exposed to light and the subsequent timing of their circadian rhythms, just as such a relationship had been found in all other species studied previously. A graph that shows this relationship is known as the phase-response curve, or PRC. Such relationships had been established and diagrammed for many other species. Lewy and his colleagues suggested that a similar PRC could be diagrammed for human beings as well.

Working from this hypothetical PRC, Dr. Lewy and a colleague, Dr. Serge Daan, used their predictions about the effects of bright light on human circadian rhythms to modify the symptoms of two individuals who traveled to Europe from the West Coast of the United States, a trip traversing nine time zones. They treated one with a regimen of light and darkness that, according to their proposed PRC, should enhance adaptation to the new time zone, and the other with a regimen calculated to delay adaptation. Their predictions were borne out when the first of the two subjects adjusted to the new time zone within six days whereas the second took more than twelve days to adjust.

Dr. Norman Rosenthal and his colleagues at the National Institute of Mental Health also used knowledge of the human PRC to shift the rhythms of people with a sleep disorder in which sleep and wake times were abnormally delayed. These individuals had a kind of "jet lag" even though they hadn't gone anywhere. By exposing themselves to bright light in the morning and restricting their exposure to bright light in the afternoon and evening, these individuals were able to shift their sleep-wake cycle to more conventional hours.

Recent studies by Drs. Czeisler and Kronauer and by Drs. Minors and Waterhouse have confirmed the existence of a PRC in human beings, which is similar to the PRC predicted by Lewy and his colleagues. On the basis of their human studies, which were patterned on animal experiments, Czeisler and his colleagues have described a strategy for shifting circadian rhythms that is fundamentally different from the techniques we will be recommending in this book. Their particular strategy involves using light at a time of day that is calculated to flatten an individual's circadian rhythms. Once flattened, the rhythms can then be reset to new times by exposing the individual to light and to darkness at certain specific times. Ongoing studies suggest that there may be no difference in the efficiency of this newer method as compared with the more established techniques for shifting circadian rhythms, used initially by Daan and Lewy and now by us in this book.

We will provide specific guidelines as to how you can use an understanding of the PRC to determine when to expose yourself to light and when to avoid it in order to minimize your symptoms of jet lag. It is important that these interventions be carried out at just the right times, since exposure to light (or darkness) at the wrong times can actually have the undesirable effect of making your jet lag worse and delaying your adjustment to the new time zone. Later in this book, you will find guidelines to the optimal times for being exposed to light and to darkness, depending on how many time zones you will cross in your particular journey, and in which direction.

In human beings, as in other animals, exposure to light in the early part of the night tends to *delay* circadian rhythms—that is, to push them *later* so that one wants to go to sleep later. On the other hand, exposure to light in the later part of the night and early part of the morning tends to *advance* circadian rhythms—that is, to push them *earlier* so that one wants to go to sleep earlier. At some time during the night the so-called switch-point occurs—the point that separates the time when light delays circadian rhythms and the time when light advances them. In most people the switch-point of the PRC probably occurs around 4:00 A.M., although in some people it will be earlier and in others later. Just *before* the switch-point is the time when exposure to light leads to the most profound *delays* in circadian rhythms. In other words, if you are exposed to bright light at, say, 3:00 A.M., then, over the ensuing days, you will tend to wake up and go to sleep *later* than you would otherwise have done. Conversely, just *after* the switch-point is the time when exposure to light leads to the most profound *advances.* In other words, if you are exposed to bright light at, say, 5:00 A.M., then over the ensuing days you will tend to go to sleep and wake up *earlier* than you would otherwise have done. Clearly then, an understanding of this switch-point, and the opposite circadian effects of exposure to light on either side of it, is central to developing strategies for averting or minimizing the jet lag that ordinarily occurs after you fly across time zones.

Although 4:00 A.M. represents an average figure for the switch-point of the PRC in humans, this varies from individual to individual. Those people who tend to go to sleep and wake up much later than most—so-called evening types or night owls—probably have a switch-point somewhat later than 4:00 A.M. Conversely, extreme morning types, who like to go to sleep and wake up earlier than most others, probably have a switch-point somewhat earlier than 4:00 A.M. The specific guidelines for helping you overcome the symptoms of jet lag are geared toward people with typical sleep-wake patterns. If you happen to be an extreme evening or morning type, be sure to consult the special section (page 26) that will help you modify these instructions to suit the particular pattern of your circadian rhythms.

Assuming that the switch-point of your PRC falls at about 4:00 A.M., when you fly across time zones and reach your destination, your switch-point (like the rest of your internal body rhythms) will remain in its old time position, at least initially. It will therefore not immediately be at 4:00 A.M. in the new time zone but either later or earlier, depending on whether you have flown east or west. Take, for instance, a flight from New York to London, an eastward trip across five time zones. On the day you arrive in London, your switch-point will fall at approximately 9:00 A.M. London time (equivalent to 4:00 A.M. in New York). When you arrive in London, you will need to shift your circadian rhythms five hours *earlier* to adjust to local time; that is, you will need to go to sleep and wake up six hours earlier than you would have had you never left New York. During the first few days after arriving in London, light exposure *after* 9:00 A.M. London time will *advance* your body clock and help you to accomplish that task. On the other hand, light exposure *before* 9:00 A.M. London time (especially just before 9:00 A.M.) will have an opposite and undesirable effect of *delaying* your body clock. By delaying your circadian rhythms further, exposure to light before 9:00 A.M. London time will slow down your adjustment to your new time zone and make your jet lag worse by making you want to go to sleep even later than you would have gone to sleep while you were in New York. Thus, you should avoid being exposed to light before 9:00 A.M. in the new time zone on the day of your arrival, which will help your rhythms adjust and shorten the duration of your jet lag symptoms. As this example illustrates, avoidance of light at certain times can be as useful in the treatment of jet lag as exposure to light at other times.

Consider the opposite situation—that is, a flight from London to New York by a traveler whose biological clock is adjusted to London time. This flight involves a five hour time shift in a westward direction. On arrival in New York the switch-point in your PRC will now be at 11:00 P.M. New York time (equivalent to 4:00 A.M. London time). On arrival in the United States you will need to shift your rhythms five hours *later* to adjust to local time; that is, you will need to go to sleep and wake up five hours later than you would have had you never left London. In the few days after you arrive in New York, light exposure in the early evening, *before* 11:00 P.M. New York time, will help you do that by shifting your rhythms *later,* whereas light exposure *after* 11:00 P.M. New York time will shift your rhythms in the wrong direction (earlier), thereby slowing down your adjustment to the new time zone. You should try *not* to be exposed to bright light after 11:00 P.M. New York time, a task that is not too difficult since the sun already will have set.

Further guidelines about how best to adjust to the rhythm shifts resulting from the two particular trips mentioned above are provided on pages 41 and 93, in the section containing instructions for all possible flights. Trips that involve crossing only one or two time zones do not generally produce significant jet lag and, for that reason, we have not provided special instructions for them. As you might expect, the specifics as to when you should be exposed to light and dark will be determined by the particular flight you take, since it will depend on the number of time zones you cross and the direction in which you are traveling.

At this point, it would be useful to understand what it means to be exposed to light or to darkness.

Being in the Light and in the Dark

Light exerts its influence on the biological clock via direct nerve connections between the eyes and the brain. It is important to understand this because when we refer to being in the light, we mean having light enter the eyes. Being in the dark refers to having very little light enter the eyes. So if you are tanning outside on a sunny day with a blindfold over your eyes, that would, paradoxically, constitute being in the dark as far as this manual is concerned. It is the exposure of your eyes to light or to darkness that influences your circadian rhythms and therefore affects your adjustment to a new time zone.

We will refer many times to being in the light and being in the dark. It is important for you to understand exactly what we mean by these terms. The brighter the light and the darker the dark, the more powerful are their influences on your biological clock. We therefore recommend that at the designated times you be exposed to light as bright as possible and to darkness as dark as possible *within safe guidelines.* In most circumstances, however, it should be possible to apply the guidelines in this manual without any risk.

Although we suggest that you be in bright light, it is important *never to stare directly at the sun or at very bright incandescent lights,* such as halogen lights, since this may be

Important Safety Note
The issue of safety is naturally of paramount importance. Safety considerations should be borne in mind when you are in both light and dark conditions.

harmful to the eyes. Artificial light that is not diffused by a screen is concentrated in very bright "hot spots" that can injure the eyes. In addition, some people suffer from certain eye conditions, particularly those involving the retina, that can be made worse by bright light. If you believe you may be suffering from such an eye problem, be sure to consult your doctor before exposing your eyes to bright light of any type.

Similarly, *be sure not to engage in activities that could be potentially dangerous when in the dark,* or when you are wearing dark glasses. This could apply, for example, to driving or to walking down a staircase (or descending an escalator) with your luggage in hand, when the surrounding light levels are low. Under such circumstances, there might be a risk of not noticing a car or a person on the road, or of falling down the stairs or the escalator. In all situations, considerations of safety should be given priority over those related to minimizing the symptoms of jet lag. Thus, always take off your dark glasses, even during the times when we recommend that you wear them, if, by wearing them, you would be unable to see properly and thereby expose yourself or others to any danger.

In summary, avoiding jet lag is desirable, but avoiding accidents or injury to the eyes must always take precedence.

Being in the Light

Whenever we recommend that you be in the light, the brighter the environment the more effect it is likely to have on your circadian rhythms. Indirect natural sunlight is the best type of bright light for resetting your biological clock and helping you to overcome jet lag. It is often possible to be exposed to natural sunlight at those times when such exposure will help you avoid jet lag; such sunlight is available through the window of the plane while you are traveling, through airport windows while you are waiting for a connection, or out of doors. An understanding of when you're likely to benefit from sunlight might influence your choice of a window seat on the plane or your decision to stand near a window or go outdoors when waiting for a connection or when you reach your destination.

Occasionally we will recommend that you be exposed to bright light at times when it is not possible to have direct access to sunlight, either because it is nighttime outside or because you are indoors and away from windows. On such occasions, you will need to improvise with artificial light. There may be certain brightly lit areas to which you can go for this purpose after you arrive at your destination, such as a shopping mall, a supermarket, or the health club at your hotel. Alternatively, you might gather all the lamps in your hotel room into one part of the room and sit directly in front of them. One way to produce a brightly lit environment is to put a white reflective surface, such as a pillowcase or sheet of white paper, on a desk or tabletop so that the light from the lamps is reflected off this surface. Alternatively, you might read or watch TV surrounded by these lamps. You might even choose to sit close to a lamp shade and glance at it intermittently for 10 or 15 minutes.

Note: Just as it is dangerous to stare directly at the sun, it can also be dangerous to stare at naked incandescent light bulbs, especially halogen bulbs, for prolonged periods. Therefore, do not stare at lamps unless they have lamp shades or screens that diffuse the light evenly without "hot spots."

Frequent jet fliers might wish to consider obtaining special light fixtures that emit light that is bright enough to shift human circadian rhythms for use at those times when the instructions in this book call for exposure to light. One type of fixture is a special "light box" that contains fluorescent lamps. Another type is the "light visor," an appliance that is worn on the head like a baseball cap with special light sources installed in the visor portion. The visor is the more recent of the two types of fixtures and there is less experimental evidence at this time that the visor can shift circadian rhythms than there is for the light box. On the other hand, light boxes are rather bulky—an undesirable feature for the traveler. Modern light boxes, however, are small enough to fit in the overhead compartments of most planes. In addition, if the light box is needed to help adjust to local time *after* the return flight—for example for an American returning from Europe to the East Coast of the United States—then it may be unnecessary to carry the light box with you on your journey. The visor weighs only about a pound and is therefore very handy for the traveler. Studies of its efficacy in helping overcome jet lag are currently in progress. If it turns out to be as effective as we believe it is, it should become a very useful addition to the jet lag kit of the frequent flier.

Sources for obtaining both light boxes and the light visor are provided on pages 31–32. It is important to emphasize that none of these devices is essential in order to shift the biological clock. That can be done quite effectively merely by following the instructions in this book, which describe the use of eyemasks, dark glasses, and available light. Using the other devices—a light box or a light visor—simply makes it easier to expose yourself to sufficient levels of light when it is needed.

Being in the Dark

Whenever we recommend that you be in the dark, the darker the environment the more likely it is to have the desired effect on your circadian rhythms. If it is nighttime and you are in your own room, it should be easy to make your environment as dark as you want. In practice, though, you will often be on your journey or out and about at times when instructions in this book will direct you to be in the dark. To help you avoid light at those times of day when it is advisable for you to do so, we recommend that you wear an eyemask when you sleep or a pair of dark glasses (preferably the wrap-around type) when you're awake. Along with this manual, we are providing you with an eyemask and a set of dark glasses. For those of you who wear prescription glasses, the enclosed dark glasses can be worn underneath them.

The enclosed dark glasses are mostly, but not fully, effective in screening out light. A pair of dark wrap-around goggles would be even more effective in this regard and, should you have such a pair, feel free to use it instead of the glasses. Should you have a pair of regular dark glasses, you may achieve an optimal effect by wearing the enclosed dark glasses underneath your own set. This combination should filter out most of the light entering the eyes from outside. We must emphasize once again that if you wear dark glasses in dim indoor conditions, and especially if you wear the enclosed dark glasses under your own dark glasses, the accuracy of your vision may be greatly diminished. Therefore **do not wear the dark glasses in any situation where it is critical that you be able to see clearly**—for example, when you are driving, operating machinery, walking up or down stairs, riding on an escalator, or walking along a steep or winding path. Taking off the glasses at such times may interfere with the process of beating jet lag, but your physical safety must, of course, be your first priority.

The value of the eyemask is twofold. First, it prevents light from entering the eyes through the closed eyelids while you are asleep or trying to sleep, which will frequently be at a time when exposure to light might delay your adjustment to the new time zone and prolong your jet lag symptoms. Second, it prevents exposure to bright light upon awakening. In our specific instructions for overcoming jet lag, we will frequently suggest that you remove the eyemask and put on your dark glasses. We suggest that in order to carry out these instructions, you have your dark glasses close at hand so that you can keep your eyes shut while you switch from the eyemask to the dark glasses, thereby minimizing your exposure to light at the wrong time.

Activity and Rest

Although most research into the effects of environmental time cues in both animals and humans has focused on the role of light and darkness, there is mounting evidence that other factors also play an important role. Chief among these are activity and rest, which can therefore also be used to help you overcome jet lag. Research suggests that activity might play a role similar to that of light in shifting circadian rhythms. In attempting to minimize your jet lag, it is therefore generally desirable to be active at those times when you should be exposed to light. It is quite likely that combining light and activity may actually have a more powerful effect than each of those factors alone. One renowned circadian rhythm researcher has described how he jogs in the bright sunlight on arriving at his destination in order to hasten his circadian rhythm adjustment.

There is some evidence that being mentally alert and engaged affects the body clock in the same ways as activity and light do. This fact can be used to advantage in situations where it may be impossible to be physically active, such as when you are on the plane. In such situations, engaging in an interesting conversation or reading an exciting novel at those times when light and activity are called for may be a worthwhile strategy.

Just as activity appears to have an effect on circadian rhythms similar to that of light, so rest may work in a manner similar to darkness. We therefore recommend that you remain at rest at those times of day when you need to be exposed to darkness. In situations where you are unable to be in the dark at the required time, resting by itself may be helpful.

At certain points in the manual we suggest that you try to sleep. Don't worry if that should prove difficult or impossible, as evidence suggests that rest in itself (even without sleep) can be helpful in minimizing the effects of jet lag. We recommend therefore that if you cannot sleep, simply rest at the prescribed times.

Mealtimes, Diet, and Alcohol

There is evidence from animal studies that mealtimes have some effect on the timing of circadian rhythms. Researchers have not succeeded so far in identifying the location of the clock in the brain responsible for these effects of meals, but it seems to be quite distinct from the clock that is regulated by light and dark. Whether the timing of meals can be used to advantage to help you adjust to the time zone at your destination and thereby decrease your symptoms of jet lag remains to be seen. It would make sense, however, to eat your meals at the same time as the local residents when you reach your destination.

Much has been written in the popular press about avoiding jet lag by going on special diets. There is, unfortunately, very little scientific basis for these recommendations.

Drinking alcohol or caffeinated beverages raises potential difficulties for the traveler wishing to minimize jet lag. Once again, there is not much data about how these substances affect human circadian rhythms and adjustment following jet lag. As we have already mentioned, it is important that you be active and exposed to light at certain times, and inactive and in the dark at other times. Bear in mind when drinking caffeinated beverages that they may keep you awake and active into those times when we recommend that you be asleep or inactive.

We do not recommend the use of alcohol as a sleeping remedy because there is evidence that as the alcohol is metabolized and blood alcohol levels decrease, there is a rebound effect and sleep tends to be disrupted.

More Scientific Information
for the Irrepressibly Curious

As the title of this section suggests, it is not necessary to know anything about its contents in order to benefit from the directions for overcoming jet lag provided in this book. However, the scientifically curious reader might wish to know a bit more about the biological clock that we have mentioned repeatedly in earlier sections and how it is influenced by light and other environmental variables.

Where is the location of the main biological clock? All evidence points to the suprachiasmatic nuclei (SCN), two tiny groups of nerve cells located in the hypothalamus, a small structure that lies behind the eyes at the base of the brain. Animal experiments in which the SCN have been damaged resulted in animals with disturbed circadian rhythms. The cells of the SCN have inherent electrical rhythms of their own, and re-implanting fetal SCN cells into SCN-damaged animals can restore their normal circadian rhythms.

The SCN are linked to the retinas of the eyes by direct nerve connections through which light and dark adjust the timing of the clock. The SCN, in turn, are connected to other parts of the hypothalamus by nerve cells, through which they impart a daily rhythm to all manner of physiological and behavioral functions. The SCN are also connected to the pineal gland by a tortuous series of nerve cells that go as far down as the neck before looping back up into the head to connect to the pineal gland, which is located at the base of the brain. Through these connections, the SCN generate a regular nighttime rhythm of melatonin secretion by the pineal. It is via the nerve connections from the eyes to the SCN and from the SCN to the pineal gland that light affects melatonin secretion.

These neural signals are transmitted from one nerve to another by chemical messengers (or neurotransmitters). There are receptors for a rich array of neurotransmitters in the SCN and other parts of the hypothalamus. The list of substances known to be involved in this neural transmission, and knowledge about the distribution of the nerve fibers involved in this transmission, grows more complex year by year. Receptors for melatonin have been found in the SCN, and it may be by acting on these receptors that melatonin has its documented effect on the timing of circadian rhythms. The effects of melatonin and many other drugs on circadian rhythms are similar to those of darkness. It may be that darkness exerts its circadian effects to some extent via its effects on melatonin secretion. Alternatively, darkness and melatonin secretion, which coincide under normal circumstances, may act in concert with each other.

Circadian rhythms may be genetically determined, at least to some extent. Researchers have identified genes that regulate the circadian rhythms of fruit flies, causing different flies to have different patterns of circadian rhythms. It is quite likely that human beings differ from one another in their internally generated patterns of circadian rhythms. In fact, researchers have actually found circadian rhythm differences between individuals kept in isolation from time cues, though it is not clear whether these differences are genetically determined. It is possible that being an extreme morning or evening type may also be influenced by our genes.

There is some evidence that light may influence the SCN by turning on the expression of certain genes in their nerve cells. These genes may in turn cause certain proteins to be produced and influence the pattern of neurotransmission. There is also evidence that patterns of response to changes in environmental light have been conserved over millions of years of evolution. For example, a recent study has found that algae, single-celled plantlike organisms, show behavioral responses to changes in the length of the day under the influence of the hormone melatonin, the same hormone that plays a very similar role in orchestrating seasonal changes in mammals including, perhaps, human beings. These are rapidly developing areas of research, and the next few years promise considerable advances in our understanding of some of these questions. Luckily, however, we do not need to wait for these questions to be answered in order to benefit from information already obtained about the effects of light and dark on circadian rhythms.

The following sections will deal with some further practical questions that may arise in applying the principles in this manual.

Quick Round-Trips

"I'm flying to Europe and back in four days. What's the best way to deal with the jet lag I expect to encounter?" we've been asked. This is the sort of quick round-trip frequently undertaken by businessmen and businesswomen. For trips of three days or less, we would not generally recommend taking any special measures to deal with jet lag. When you use this jet lag guide for longer trips, you may overcome your jet lag within two or three days (instead of the usual ten to fourteen days without its assistance). On quick round-trips, however, even with the accelerated adjustment, you will no sooner have adjusted to the new time zone than it will be time to return and readjust to the original time zone again. Strategies that may be helpful in coping with quick round-trips include: (1) checking with your physician as to whether he or she feels that sleeping medication may be helpful for the few critical nights in question; (2) arranging important business meetings at your destination at times when you would have expected to be awake and alert in the time zone of origin; and (3) allowing time following your return from the trip to catch up on any sleep loss you may have suffered as a result of your travel.

By deliberately not resetting your biological rhythms to the new time zone, you will minimize the problem of jet lag on your return.

The Concorde

If you're flying on the supersonic Concorde, you're going to arrive at your destination much more rapidly than you would if you were flying on a regular plane. How does this affect any measures you should take to avoid jet lag? The answer is, not very much. Jet lag results from the difference between the time of day at your point of origin (to which your biological rhythms have been synchronized) and the time of day at your destination (to which you want to synchronize your rhythms as quickly as possible). This time-zone difference will be the same no matter how swiftly you travel between the two points. Therefore, we suggest that you adhere to the same instructions in relation to exposure to light and dark as you would if you were traveling on a regular plane. The only difference is that when you travel on the Concorde, some of the instructions in this guide that are directed toward those travelers who are still on the plane will need to be implemented after you arrive at your destination.

Special Advice for People with Unusual Sleep-Wake Patterns: "Night Owls" and "Early Morning" Types

Our directions as to when you should be exposed to light and to darkness are geared toward those individuals with typical sleep-wake patterns—that is, those who usually go to sleep between 10:00 P.M. and 12:00 A.M. and wake up between 6:00 and 8:00 A.M. Those of you whose patterns of sleeping and waking fall outside this range should adjust the directions accordingly. For example, if you usually go to sleep after 12:00 A.M., add extra time to all the instructions, hour for hour. Say your usual sleep onset time is 1:00 A.M., your usual wake-up time is 9:00 A.M., and the instructions tell you to put on dark glasses at 5:00 P.M. in the time zone of your destination, instead put on your dark glasses at 6:00 P.M. in the time zone of your destination. For those of you who normally go to sleep and wake up early, *subtract* from the times given in the directions the difference between your times of sleeping and waking and those "typical times" mentioned above.

If your sleep-wake patterns occur at usual times but you need more sleep than average—say from 10:00 P.M. to 7:30 A.M.—then adhere to the instructions in this guide without any modification.

Changing Planes and Stopovers

Airline travel often necessitates changes of planes, or at least stopovers, in midvoyage. This is particularly true for long trips traversing many time zones. We may often spend many hours at an airport waiting for a plane to enable us to continue our journey. Airport settings present challenges, as well as opportunities, for the traveler seeking to beat jet lag by following the instructions in this book.

As used here, the word *flight* actually refers to an entire trip, including all stopovers and changes of planes, from the point of departure to the final destination. The instructions for each such flight, or trip, were designed to take into account the total number of time zones traversed, east or west. Sometimes, one trip might take much longer than another trip traversing the same number of time zones in the same direction because one of those trips requires a significant amount of waiting time in one or more airports while the other doesn't. Nevertheless, the instructions in this book for that flight apply equally to both trips.

The bottom line is that, in order to beat jet lag on your particular flight, you have to follow the instructions that tell you what to do at a particular hour into your trip. If those instructions recommend that you seek or avoid light, you have to do so in the best way possible *wherever* you happen to be, whether on the plane, in an airport, or in your city of final destination.

Seeking Light in an Airport

If the instructions for your particular flight require you to seek light at a particular time, and you find yourself at that time in an airport, there are many opportunities to follow those instructions.

During the day, light is readily available at most airports. Stay near the large, plate-glass windows that are common in transit lounges, or spend time outside on an observation deck. From time to time, look up at the sky (though never directly at the sun!). When you are instructed to expose yourself to light, looking up at the sky provides a powerful time cue that will help you beat jet lag. You might also spend time reading in an area into which sunlight is streaming. If the sun is low, or if it's cloudy, it's useful to glance outside more frequently in order to make up for the diminished light.

> Important Note
> *Never* look directly at the sun! Doing so can cause serious harm to your eyes!

Should sunlight not be available, find the best-lit spot you can, even though the lighting is artificial. Often, a restaurant has lots of light; duty-free areas are also often well lit. You can influence the amount of light entering your eyes by directing your gaze to particularly bright areas in a room—for example, white, reflective walls (as opposed to a dull, gray carpet).

Avoiding Light in an Airport

When the instructions for your particular flight require you to avoid light at a particular time, they tell you to put on your dark glasses. This maneuver should be carried out at the time required whether you happen to be on the plane or in the airport (or, for that matter, in a taxi driving to your destination).

Important Note
Always put safety first! If the dark glasses make it difficult for you to see clearly enough to walk or act safely, wherever you may be, then take them off until you can wear them safely. Similarly, if dark glasses make it difficult for you to see while driving or operating machinery, take them off until you are no longer in a position in which you might endanger yourself or others. Risking jet lag is preferable to risking an accident!

Should you be waiting in the airport, make sure you have your dark glasses available so that you can put them on when required to do so by the instructions. Often, you will be instructed to keep your dark glasses on from a time while you are still on the plane until some hours later, when you are scheduled to be waiting in an airport for your next plane or when you are scheduled to be on your next plane. In such cases, if safety permits, simply wear the dark glasses as you leave the plane and enter the airport (and, if required, as you leave the airport and enter the plane for the next leg of your journey).

Being Active in an Airport

During the times you're required to seek light, it's also important to be active. Being active at those times when we suggest you be in bright light can enhance the potency of the light in helping you overcome jet lag. Try walking—briskly if possible—from lounge to lounge.

Resting in an Airport

During the times you're required to be in the dark, it is also important to rest. Resting at those times when we suggest that you be in the dark can enhance the potency of the darkness in helping you overcome jet lag. It might be helpful to find a chair in a dark location in an airport lounge, but be sure not to get too comfortable or you may miss your next plane!

Changing Your Watch in an Airport

The instructions in this book tell you to seek or avoid light at certain times. Those times are designated as being the time in your original time zone (that is, the time in the place from which you departed) or the time in the time zone of your destination (that is, the time in the place at which you will terminate your trip). Always be sure you are following the instructions for the particular time zone that is designated. In order to simplify the instructions, we occasionally ask you, especially on long flights, to change your watch to match the time zone of your destination; do so when necessary.

Often, when you are in an airport waiting for your next flight, your watch will be set to a different time zone than are the clocks in the airport, which are set to the airport's local time zone. Since your connecting plane is scheduled to depart according to local time, make sure you are aware of that time, even if your watch is still set to a different time zone. Should you want to change your watch to match the airport's local time, it would be wise to check the instructions for your flight once you board your next plane so that you can reset your watch to a time—usually your destination time—that will make it as easy as possible for you to follow the instructions.

Resources for Obtaining Lighting Appliances

As we have noted, frequent fliers may wish to purchase a special light source in order to be exposed to bright light when it is not possible to use natural sunlight. Researchers have had the most experience with special light boxes, some of which weigh as little as eight pounds. These boxes are capable of delivering the amount of light necessary to shift biological rhythms. Three leading manufacturers of such light boxes, all of whom are willing to ship their products anywhere in the United States, are listed below. For exact weights, prices, and models, we encourage you to check with the manufacturers themselves, as these change frequently.

The SunBox Company
19217 Orbit Drive, Dept. PT
Gaithersburg, MD 20879
1-800-548-3968

Apollo Light Systems, Inc.
320 West 1060 South
Orem, UT 34058
(801)-545-9667

Medic-Lite, Inc.
Yacht Club Drive
Lake Hopatcong, NJ 07849
1-800-544-4825

The newly developed portable, head-mounted light visor has the advantage of being very light (weighing about one pound) and therefore easily transportable. Anecdotal reports on its use are encouraging, but systematic studies of its potential valve in treating jet lag have yet to be done.

Bio-Brite, Inc.
7315 Wisconsin Avenue #1300W
Bethesda, MD 20814-3202.
1-800-621-LITE

The light visor is also available from the SunBox Company.

FINDING the INSTRUCTIONS for BEATING JET LAG for YOUR PARTICULAR FLIGHT

If you know the direction in which you are traveling and the number of time zones you will be crossing, consult one of the tables on the next page to locate the page on which you will find instructions for beating jet lag on your trip. If you're not sure of the number of time zones or the direction in which you are traveling, you can obtain this information from two sections of the book—the map of the world's time zones (page vi) or the Table of Cities (pages 131–37). (Because the jet lag symptoms caused by travel through only one or two time zones are minimal, we have only included instructions for flights that cross three time zones or more.)

If you choose to consult the map in order to obtain information about your flight, proceed as follows: First, find the city from which you're departing, or the one closest to it in the same time zone. Next, find the city of destination or the one closest to it in the same time zone. Count the number of time zones you will be crossing and note the direction in which you will be traveling. Then, consult the table on page 34 to locate the page that contains instructions for beating jet lag on your trip.

If you prefer to use our Table of Cities, which lists sixty common travel destinations around the globe, turn to page 131.

If You Are Traveling West to East

NUMBER OF TIME ZONES YOU WILL CROSS	INSTRUCTIONS FOR BEATING JET LAG ON PAGE
3 (Day/Eve. Flight*)	35
3 (Overnight Flight*)	37
4	39
5	41
6	45
7	49
8	54
9	60
10	66
11	73
12	80

If You Are Traveling East to West

NUMBER OF TIME ZONES YOU WILL CROSS	INSTRUCTIONS FOR BEATING JET LAG ON PAGE
3	88
4	91
5	93
6	96
7	99
8	102
9	106
10	111
11	116
12	120
13	125

*The instructions for flying eastward across three time zones differ depending on whether one flies during the day/evening or overnight. Be sure to consult the correct set of instructions.

THREE TIME ZONES EAST—DAYTIME OR EVENING FLIGHT

For example:
From the U.S. West Coast to the U.S. East Coast

I.

Board plane for take-off.

2.

After about five hours, the plane has crossed three time zones and lands. Do not wear dark glasses; exposure to light at this time is not a problem.

3.

FIRST NIGHT AT DESTINATION: Try to go to bed before midnight, local time. Avoid the tendency to stay awake past midnight. After midnight, staying awake, being exposed to light, and being active will interfere with beating jet lag. Before going to bed, put on a cloth eyemask, and have your dark glasses available so that you can put them on in place of the

mask when you get out of bed during the night or in the morning.

4.

FIRST MORNING AT DESTINATION: If you
arise before 7 A.M., be sure to put on
your dark glasses when you take off
your eyemask. Avoiding early morning light by wearing either the eyemask or the dark glasses until 7 A.M.
will help you beat jet lag. Be careful
as you walk with the glasses on.
NOTE: Don't wear the dark glasses if
the light level is too low for them to
be worn safely.

5.

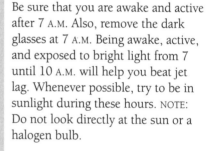

Be sure that you are awake and active
after 7 A.M. Also, remove the dark
glasses at 7 A.M. Being awake, active,
and exposed to bright light from 7
until 10 A.M. will help you beat jet
lag. Whenever possible, try to be in
sunlight during these hours. NOTE:
Do not look directly at the sun or a
halogen bulb.

6.

It's best not to nap during the day or
evening so that you can get a full
night's sleep at the end of the day.
If you wish to nap, do so between
2 and 7 P.M. and keep your nap as
short as possible.

THREE TIME ZONES EAST—OVERNIGHT FLIGHT

For example:
From the U.S. West Coast to the U.S. East Coast

1. Board plane for take-off.

2. After 10 P.M. in your original time zone, being exposed to light will interfere with beating jet lag. Therefore, at 10 P.M. in your original time zone, put on the dark glasses. If you expect to be asleep at 10 P.M., put on the cloth eyemask before going to sleep. When you wake up, be sure to put on the dark glasses when you take off the eyemask.

3.   FIRST MORNING AT DESTINATION: After about five hours, the plane has crossed three time zones and lands. Be sure to continue to wear the dark glasses and be as inactive as possible until 7 A.M. in the time zone of your destination. Before 7 A.M., being exposed to light and being active will interfere with beating jet lag. Be careful as you walk with the glasses on.

4.

After 7 A.M. in the time zone of your destination, especially from 7 to 10 A.M., exposure to light will help you beat jet lag. Remove the dark glasses or eyemask. If possible, maximize your exposure to sunlight during these hours. NOTE: Do not look directly at the sun or a halogen bulb. If you are flying during this period, try to sit next to a window. If you are on the ground, try to be out of doors as much as possible. If indoors, try to stay near a window or in a brightly illuminated room.

You are likely to be tired during the first day at your destination, but this will be due to lack of a full night's sleep rather than to jet lag. It's best not to nap during the day or evening so that you can get a full night's sleep at the end of the day. If you wish to nap, do so between 2 and 7 P.M. and keep your nap as short as possible.

5.

FIRST NIGHT AT DESTINATION: Try to go to bed before midnight, local time. Avoid the tendency to stay awake past midnight. After midnight, staying awake, being exposed to light, and being active will interfere with beating jet lag.

6.

SECOND MORNING AT DESTINATION: Arise at the time that will be customary during your stay at your destination. Avoid sleeping late. Being active and exposed to bright light at the beginning of the day will help you lock in to local time.

FOUR TIME ZONES EAST

For example:
From Hawaii to the U.S. Midwest

1.

Board plane for take-off.

2.

FIRST DAY OF TRAVEL: After 10 P.M. in your original time zone, being exposed to light will interfere with your effort to beat jet lag. Therefore, at 10 P.M. in your original time zone put on the dark glasses. If you would expect to be asleep at 10 P.M. in your original time zone (2 A.M. in the destination time zone), put on the cloth eyemask before going to sleep. When you wake up, be sure to put on the dark glasses when you take off the eyemask.

3.

FIRST MORNING AT DESTINATION: After about six hours, the plane has crossed four time zones and lands. Be sure to continue to wear the dark glasses and be as inactive as possible until 8 A.M. in the time zone of your destination. Before 8 A.M., being exposed to light and being active will interfere with your effort to beat jet lag. Be careful as you walk with the glasses on. NOTE: Don't wear the dark glasses if the light level is too low for them to be worn safely.

4.

At 8 A.M. in the time zone of your destination, remove the dark glasses or the eyemask. After 8 A.M., especially from 8 to 11 A.M., exposure to light and being active will help you beat jet lag. If possible, maximize your exposure to sunlight during these hours (never stare directly at the sun!). If you are flying during this period, try to sit next to a window. If you are on the ground, try to be out of doors as much as possible. If indoors, try to stay near a window or in a brightly illuminated room.

You are likely to be tired during the first day at your destination, but this will probably be due to lack of a full night's sleep rather than to jet lag. It's best not to nap during the day or evening, so that you can get a full night's sleep at the end of the day. If you wish to nap, do so between 2 and 8 P.M., and keep your nap as short as possible.

5.

FIRST NIGHT AT DESTINATION: Try to go to bed between 10 P.M. and midnight, local time. Avoid the tendency to stay awake past midnight. After midnight, staying awake, being exposed to light, and being active will interfere with your effort to beat jet lag.

6.

SECOND MORNING AT DESTINATION: Arise at the time that will be customary during your stay at your destination. Avoid sleeping late. Being active and exposed to bright light in the morning will help you lock in to local time. NOTE: Do not look directly at the sun or a halogen bulb.

FIVE TIME ZONES EAST

For example:
From the U.S. East Coast to England

1.

TO AIRPLANE

Board plane for take-off.

2.

After 10 P.M. in your original time zone, being exposed to light will interfere with your effort to beat jet lag. Therefore, at 10 P.M. in your original time zone, put on the dark glasses. NOTE: Don't wear the dark glasses if the light level is too low for them to be worn safely. If you expect to be asleep at 10 P.M., put on the cloth eyemask before going to sleep. When you wake up, be sure to put on the dark glasses when you take off the eyemask.

3.

FIRST MORNING AT DESTINATION: After about seven hours, the plane has crossed five time zones and lands. Be sure to continue to wear the dark glasses and be as inactive as possible until 9 A.M. in the time zone of your destination. Until 9 A.M., being exposed to light and being active will interfere with your effort to beat jet lag. Be careful as you walk with the glasses on. NOTE: Don't wear the dark glasses if the light level is too low for them to be worn safely.

4.

At 9 A.M. in the time zone of your destination, remove the dark glasses or eyemask. After 9 A.M., especially from 9 A.M. to noon, exposure to light and being active will help you beat jet lag. If possible, maximize your exposure to sunlight during these hours. NOTE: Do not look directly at the sun or a halogen bulb.

If you are flying during this period, try to sit next to a window. If you are on the ground, try to be out of doors as much as possible. If indoors, try to stay near a window or in a brightly illuminated room.

You are likely to be tired during the first day at your destination, but this will be due to lack of a full night's sleep rather than to jet lag. It's best not to nap during the day or evening, so that you can get a full night's sleep at the end of the day. If you wish to nap, do so between 2 and 8 P.M., and keep your nap as short as possible.

5.

FIRST NIGHT AT DESTINATION: Try to go to bed between 9 P.M. and midnight, local time. Avoid the tendency to stay awake past midnight. After midnight, staying awake, being exposed to light, and being active will interfere with your effort to beat jet lag. Before going to bed, close the curtains, put on a cloth eyemask, and have your dark glasses available so that you can put them on in place of the mask when you get out of bed during the night or in the morning. NOTE: Don't wear the dark glasses if the light level is too low for them to be worn safely.

6.

SECOND MORNING AT DESTINATION: Sleeping or remaining inactive until 7 A.M. would be helpful. If you arise before 7 A.M., be sure that you replace your eyemask with the dark glasses. Avoiding early morning light by wearing either the eyemask or the dark glasses until 7 A.M. will help you beat jet lag. Be careful as you walk with the glasses on. NOTE: Don't wear the dark glasses if the light level is too low for them to be worn safely.

7.

Be sure that you are awake and active after 7 A.M. Also, remove the dark glasses at 7 A.M. Being awake, active, and exposed to bright light from 7 until 10 A.M. will help you beat jet lag. If possible, maximize your exposure to sunlight. NOTE: Do not look directly at the sun or a halogen bulb. Try to be out of doors as much as possible. If indoors, try to stay near a window or in a brightly illuminated room.

8.

SECOND NIGHT AT DESTINATION: Try to go to bed before midnight, local time. After midnight, staying awake, being exposed to light, and being active will interfere with your effort to beat jet lag.

9.

THIRD MORNING AT DESTINATION: Arise at the time that will be customary during your stay at your destination. Avoid sleeping late. Being active and exposed to bright light in the morning will help you lock in to local time. NOTE: Do not look directly at the sun or a halogen bulb.

SIX TIME ZONES EAST

For example:
From the U.S. East Coast to Western Europe

1.

Board plane for take-off.

2.

After 10 P.M. in your original time zone, being exposed to light will interfere with your effort to beat jet lag. Therefore, wherever you are at 10 P.M. in your original time zone, put on the dark glasses. If you expect to be asleep at 10 P.M., put on the cloth eyemask before going to sleep. When you wake up, be sure to put on the dark glasses when you take off the eyemask. Be careful as you

walk with the glasses on. NOTE: Don't wear the dark glasses if the light level is too low for them to be worn safely.

3.

FIRST MORNING AT DESTINATION: After about eight hours, the plane has crossed six time zones and lands. Be sure to continue to wear the dark glasses and be as inactive as possible until 10 A.M. in the time zone of your destination. Until 10 A.M., being exposed to light and being active will interfere with your effort to beat jet lag. Be careful as you walk with the glasses on.

4.

At 10 A.M. in the time zone of your destination, remove the dark glasses or eyemask. After 10 A.M., especially from 10 A.M. to 1 P.M., exposure to light and being active will help you beat jet lag. If possible, maximize your exposure to sunlight during these hours. NOTE: Do not look directly at the sun or a halogen bulb. If you are flying during this period, try to sit next to a window. If you are on the ground, try to be out of doors as much as possible. If indoors, try to stay near a window or in a brightly illuminated room.

You are likely to be tired during the first day at your destination, but this will be due to lack of a full night's sleep rather than to jet lag. It's best not to nap during the day or evening, so that you can get a full night's sleep at the end of the day. If you wish to nap, do so between 2 and 8 P.M., and keep your nap as short as possible.

5.

FIRST NIGHT AT DESTINATION: Try to go to bed between 9 P.M. and midnight, local time. Avoid the tendency to stay awake past midnight. After midnight, staying awake, being exposed to light, and being active will interfere with your effort to beat jet lag. Before going to bed, close the curtains, put on a cloth eyemask, and have your dark glasses available so that you can put them on in place of the mask when you get out of bed during the night or in the morning.

6.

SECOND MORNING AT DESTINATION: Sleeping or remaining inactive until 8 A.M. would be helpful. If you arise before 8 A.M., be sure that you replace your eyemask with the dark glasses. Avoiding early morning light by wearing either the eyemask or the dark glasses until 8 A.M. will help you beat jet lag. Be careful as you walk with the glasses on. NOTE: Don't wear the dark glasses if the light level is too low for them to be worn safely.

7.

Be sure that you are awake and active after 8 A.M. Also, remove the dark glasses at 8 A.M. Being awake, active, and exposed to bright light from 8 until 11 A.M. will help you beat jet lag. If possible, maximize your exposure to sunlight. NOTE: Do not look directly at the sun or a halogen bulb. Try to be out of doors as much as possible. If indoors, try to stay near a window or in a brightly illuminated room.

8.

SECOND NIGHT AT DESTINATION: Try to go to bed before midnight, local time. After midnight, staying awake, being exposed to light, and being active will interfere with your effort to beat jet lag.

9.

THIRD MORNING AT DESTINATION: Arise at the time that will be customary during your stay at your destination. Avoid sleeping late. Being active and exposed to bright light in the morning will help you lock in to local time. NOTE: Do not look directly at the sun or a halogen bulb.

SEVEN TIME ZONES EAST

For example:
From the U.S. Midwest to Western Europe

1.

Board plane for take-off.

2.

After 10 P.M. in your original time zone, being exposed to light will interfere with your effort to beat jet lag. Therefore, wherever you are at

10 P.M. in your original time zone, put on the dark glasses. If you expect to be asleep at 10 P.M., put on the cloth eyemask before going to sleep. When you wake up, be sure to put on the dark glasses when you take off the eyemask. Be careful as you walk with the glasses on. NOTE: Don't wear the dark glasses if the light level is too low for them to be worn safely.

3.

FIRST MORNING AT DESTINATION: After about nine hours, the plane has crossed seven time zones and lands. Be sure to continue to wear the dark glasses and be as inactive as possible until 11 A.M. in the time zone of your destination. Until 11 A.M., being exposed to light and being active will interfere with your effort to beat jet lag. Be careful as you walk with the glasses on. NOTE: Don't wear the dark glasses if the light level is too low for them to be worn safely.

4.

At 11 A.M. in the time zone of your destination, remove the dark glasses or eyemask. After 11 A.M., especially from 11 A.M. to 2 P.M., exposure to light and being active will help you beat jet lag. If possible, maximize your exposure to sunlight during these hours. NOTE: Do not look directly at the sun or a halogen bulb. If you are flying during this period, try to sit next to a window. If you are on the ground, try to be out of doors

as much as possible. If indoors, try to stay near a window or in a brightly illuminated room.

You are likely to be tired during the first day at your destination, but this will be due to lack of a full night's sleep rather than to jet lag. It's best not to nap during the day or evening, so that you can get a full night's sleep at the end of the day. If you wish to nap, do so between 3 and 8 P.M., and keep your nap as short as possible.

5.

FIRST NIGHT AT DESTINATION: Try to go to bed between 9 P.M. and midnight, local time. Avoid the tendency to stay awake past midnight. After midnight, staying awake, being exposed to light, and being active will interfere with your effort to beat jet lag. Before going to bed, close the curtains, put on a cloth eyemask, and have your dark glasses available so that you can put them on in place of the mask when you get out of bed during the night or in the morning.

6.

SECOND MORNING AT DESTINATION: Sleeping or remaining inactive until 9 A.M. would be helpful. If you arise before 9 A.M., be sure that you replace your eyemask with the dark glasses. Avoiding early morning light by wearing either the eyemask or dark glasses until 9 A.M. will help you beat jet lag. Be careful as you

walk with the glasses on. NOTE: Don't wear the dark glasses if the light level is too low for them to be worn safely.

7.

Be sure that you are awake and active after 9 A.M. Also, remove the dark glasses at 9 A.M. Being awake, active, and exposed to bright light from 9 A.M. until noon will help you beat jet lag. If possible, maximize your exposure to sunlight. NOTE: Do not look directly at the sun or a halogen bulb. Try to be out of doors as much as possible. If indoors, try to stay near a window or in a brightly illuminated room.

8.

SECOND NIGHT AT DESTINATION: Try to go to bed before midnight, local time. After midnight, staying awake, being exposed to light, and being active will interfere with your effort to beat jet lag.

If you plan to arise earlier than 7 A.M., then before going to bed, close the curtains, put on a cloth eyemask, and have your dark glasses available so that you can put them on in place of the mask when you get out of bed during the night or in the morning.

9.

THIRD MORNING AT DESTINATION: If you arise before 7 A.M., be sure that you replace your eyemask with the dark glasses. Avoiding early morning light by wearing either the eyemask or dark glasses until 7 A.M. will help you beat jet lag. Be careful as you walk with the glasses on. NOTE: Don't wear the dark glasses if the light level is too low for them to be worn safely.

10.

Be sure that you are awake and active after 7 A.M. Also, remove the dark glasses at 7 A.M.. Being awake, active, and exposed to bright light from 7 until 10 A.M. will help you beat jet lag. If possible, maximize your exposure to sunlight during these hours. NOTE: Do not look directly at the sun or a halogen bulb. Try to be out of doors as much as possible. If indoors, try to stay near a window or in a brightly illuminated room.

It's best not to nap during the day or evening, so that you can get a full night's sleep at the end of the day. If you wish to nap, do so between 3 and 8 P.M., and keep your nap as short as possible.

II.

THIRD NIGHT AT DESTINATION: Try to go to bed before midnight, local time. After midnight, staying awake, being exposed to light, and being active will interfere with your effort to beat jet lag.

12.

FOURTH MORNING AT DESTINATION: Arise at the time that will be customary during your stay at your destination. Avoid sleeping late. Being active and exposed to bright light in the morning will help you lock in to local time.

EIGHT TIME ZONES EAST

For example:
From the U.S. West Coast to England

I.

Board plane for take-off.

2.

After 10 P.M. in your original time zone, being exposed to light will interfere with your effort to beat jet lag. Therefore, wherever you are at 10 P.M. in your original time zone, put on the dark glasses. If you expect to be asleep at 10 P.M., put on the cloth eyemask before going to sleep. When you wake up, be sure to put on the dark glasses when you take off the eyemask. Be careful as you walk with the glasses on. NOTE: Don't wear the dark glasses if the light level is too low for them to be worn safely.

3.

FIRST MORNING EN ROUTE OR AT DESTINATION: Whether you are en route to your destination or have finished crossing eight time zones and have arrived at your destination, be sure to continue to wear the dark glasses, be as inactive as possible, and try to sleep, until 4 A.M. in your original time zone (noon in the time zone of your destination). Until this time, being exposed to light and being active will interfere with your effort to beat jet lag. Be careful as you walk with the glasses on. NOTE: Don't wear the dark glasses if the light level is too low for them to be worn safely.

4.

At 4 A.M. in your original time zone, remove the dark glasses or eyemask. After 4 A.M., especially from 4 to 7 A.M., exposure to light and being

active will help you beat jet lag. If possible, maximize your exposure to sunlight during these hours. NOTE: Do not look directly at the sun or a halogen bulb. If you are flying during this period, try to sit next to a window. If you are on the ground, try to be out of doors as much as possible. If indoors, try to stay near a window or in a brightly illuminated room.

You are likely to be tired during the first day at your destination, but this will be due to lack of a full night's sleep rather than to jet lag.

It's best not to nap during the day or evening, so that you can get a full night's sleep at the end of the day. If you wish to nap, do so between 4 and 8 P.M. in the time zone of your destination, and keep your nap as short as possible.

5.

FIRST NIGHT AT DESTINATION: Try to go to bed between 10 P.M. and midnight, local time. Avoid the tendency to stay awake past midnight. After midnight, staying awake, being exposed to light, and being active will interfere with your effort to beat jet lag. Before going to bed, close the curtains, put on a cloth eyemask, and have your dark glasses available so that you can put them on in place of the mask when you get out of bed during the night or in the morning.

6.

SECOND MORNING AT DESTINATION: Sleeping or remaining inactive until 10 A.M. would be helpful. If you arise before 10 A.M., be sure that you replace your eyemask with the dark glasses. Avoiding early morning light by wearing either the eyemask or dark glasses until 10 A.M. will help you beat jet lag. Be careful as you walk with the glasses on. NOTE: Don't wear the dark glasses if the light level is too low for them to be worn safely.

7.

Be sure that you are awake and active after 10 A.M. Also, remove the dark glasses at 10 A.M. Being awake, active, and exposed to bright light from 10 A.M. until 1 P.M. will help you beat jet lag. If possible, maximize your exposure to sunlight during these hours. NOTE: Do not look directly at the sun or a halogen bulb. Try to be out of doors as much as possible. If indoors, try to stay near a window or in a brightly illuminated room.

It's best not to nap during the day or evening, so that you can get a full night's sleep at the end of the day. If you wish to nap, do so between 2 and 8 P.M., and keep your nap as short as possible.

8.

SECOND NIGHT AT DESTINATION: Try to go to bed before midnight. Avoid the tendency to stay awake past midnight. After midnight, staying awake, being exposed to light, and being active will interfere with your effort to beat jet lag. Before going to bed, close the curtains, put on a cloth eyemask, and have your dark glasses available so that you can put them on in place of the mask when you get out of bed during the night or in the morning.

9.

THIRD MORNING AT DESTINATION: Sleeping or remaining inactive until 8 A.M. would be helpful. If you arise before 8 A.M., be sure that you replace your eyemask with the dark glasses. Avoiding early morning light by wearing either the eyemask or dark glasses until 8 A.M. will help you beat jet lag. Be careful as you walk with the glasses on. NOTE: Don't wear the dark glasses if the light level is too low for them to be worn safely.

10.

Be sure that you are awake and active after 8 A.M. Also, remove the dark glasses at 8 A.M. Being awake, active, and exposed to bright light from 8 until 11 A.M. will help you beat jet lag. If possible, maximize your exposure to sunlight during these hours. NOTE: Do not look directly at the sun or a halogen bulb. Try to be out of doors as much as possible. If indoors, try to stay near a window or in a brightly illuminated room.

It's best not to nap during the day or evening, so that you can get a full night's sleep at the end of the day. If you wish to nap, do so between 2 and 8 P.M., and keep your nap as short as possible.

II.

THIRD NIGHT AT DESTINATION: Try to go to bed before midnight. After midnight, staying awake, being exposed to light, and being active will interfere with your effort to beat jet lag.

I2.

FOURTH MORNING AT DESTINATION: Arise at the time that will be customary during your stay at your destination. Avoid sleeping late. Being active and exposed to bright light in the morning will help you lock in to local time.

NINE TIME ZONES EAST

For example:
From the U.S. West Coast to Western Europe

I.

Board plane for take-off.

2.

After 10 P.M. in your original time zone, being exposed to light will interfere with your effort to beat jet lag. Therefore, wherever you are at 10 P.M. in your original time zone, put on the dark glasses. If you expect to be asleep at 10 P.M., put on the cloth eyemask before going to sleep. When you wake up, be sure to put on the dark glasses when you take off the eyemask. Be careful as you walk with the glasses on. NOTE: Don't wear the dark glasses if the light level is too low for them to be worn safely.

3.

FIRST MORNING EN ROUTE OR AT DESTI-NATION: Whether you are en route to your destination or have finished crossing nine time zones and have arrived at your destination, be sure to continue to wear the dark glasses, be as inactive as possible, and try to sleep until 4 A.M. in your original time zone (1 P.M. in the time zone of your destination). Until this time, being exposed to light and being active will interfere with your effort to beat jet lag. Be careful as you walk with the glasses on. NOTE: Don't wear the dark glasses if the light level is too low for them to be worn safely.

4.

At 4 A.M. in your original time zone, remove the dark glasses or the eyemask. After 4 A.M., especially from 4 to 7 A.M., exposure to light and being active will help you beat jet lag. If possible, maximize your exposure to sunlight during these hours. NOTE: Do not look directly at the sun or a halogen bulb. If you are flying during this period, try to sit next to a window. If you are on the ground, try to be out of doors as much as possible. If indoors, try to stay near a window or in a brightly illuminated room.

You are likely to be tired during the first day at your destination, but this will be due to lack of a full night's sleep rather than to jet lag.

It's best not to nap during the day or evening, so that you can get a full night's sleep at the end of the day. If you wish to nap, do so between 5 and 9 P.M. in the time zone of your destination, and keep your nap as short as possible.

5.

FIRST NIGHT AT DESTINATION: Try to go to bed between 10 P.M. and 1 A.M., local time. Avoid the tendency to stay awake past 1 A.M. After 1 A.M., staying awake, being exposed to light, and being active will interfere with your effort to beat jet lag. Before going to bed, close the curtains, put on a cloth eyemask, and have your dark glasses available so that you can put them on in place of the mask when you get out of bed during the night or in the morning.

6.

SECOND MORNING AT DESTINATION: Sleeping or remaining inactive until 11 A.M. would be helpful. If you arise before 11 A.M., be sure that you replace your eyemask with the dark glasses. Avoiding early morning light by wearing either the eyemask or dark glasses until 11 A.M. will help you beat jet lag. Be careful as you walk with the glasses on. NOTE: Don't wear the dark glasses if the light level is too low for them to be worn safely.

7.

Be sure that you are awake and active after 11 A.M. Also, remove the dark glasses at 11 A.M. Being awake, active, and exposed to bright light from 11 A.M. until 2 P.M. will help you beat jet lag. If possible, maximize your exposure to sunlight during these hours. NOTE: Do not look directly at the sun or a halogen bulb. Try to be out of doors as much as possible. If indoors, try to stay near a window or in a brightly illuminated room.

It's best not to nap during the day or evening, so that you can get a full night's sleep at the end of the day. If you wish to nap, do so between 2 and 9 P.M., and keep your nap as short as possible.

8.

SECOND NIGHT AT DESTINATION: Try to go to bed before midnight. Avoid the tendency to stay awake past midnight. After midnight, staying awake, being exposed to light, and being active will interfere with your effort to beat jet lag. Before going to bed, close the curtains, put on a cloth eyemask, and have your dark glasses available so that you can put them on in place of the mask when you get out of bed during the night or in the morning.

9.

THIRD MORNING AT DESTINATION: Sleeping or remaining inactive until 9 A.M. would be helpful. If you arise before 9 A.M., be sure that you replace your eyemask with the dark glasses. Avoiding early morning light by wearing either the eyemask or dark glasses until 9 A.M. will help you beat jet lag. Be careful as you walk with the glasses on. NOTE: Don't wear the dark glasses if the light level is too low for them to be worn safely.

10.

Be sure that you are awake and active after 9 A.M. Also, remove the dark glasses at 9 A.M. Being awake, active, and exposed to bright light from 9 A.M. until noon will help you beat jet lag. If possible, maximize your exposure to sunlight during these hours. NOTE: Do not look directly at the sun or a halogen bulb. Try to be out of doors as much as possible. If indoors, try to stay near a window or in a brightly illuminated room.

It's best not to nap during the day or evening, so that you can get a full night's sleep at the end of the day. If you wish to nap, do so between 2 and 9 P.M., and keep your nap as short as possible.

11.

THIRD NIGHT AT DESTINATION: Try to go to bed before midnight. After midnight, staying awake, being exposed to light, and being active will interfere with your effort to beat jet lag. If you plan to arise earlier than 7 A.M., then before going to bed, close the curtains, put on a cloth eyemask, and have your dark glasses available so that you can put them on in place of the mask when you get out of bed during the night or in the morning.

12.

FOURTH MORNING AT DESTINATION: Sleeping or remaining inactive until 7 A.M. would be helpful. If you arise before 7 A.M., be sure that you replace your eyemask with the dark glasses. Avoiding early morning light by wearing either the eyemask or dark glasses until 7 A.M. will help you beat jet lag. Be careful as you walk with the glasses on. NOTE: Don't wear the dark glasses if the light level is too low for them to be worn safely.

13.

Be sure that you are awake and active after 7 A.M. Also, remove the dark glasses at 7 A.M. Being awake, active, and exposed to bright light from 7 until 10 A.M. will help you beat jet lag. If possible, maximize your exposure to sunlight during these hours. NOTE: Do not look directly at the sun or a halogen bulb. Try to be out of doors as much as possible. If indoors, try to stay near a window or in a brightly illuminated room.

It's best not to nap during the day or evening, so that you can get a full night's sleep at the end of the day. If you wish to nap, do so between 11 A.M. and 9 P.M., and keep your nap as short as possible.

14.

FOURTH NIGHT AT DESTINATION: Try to go to bed before midnight. After midnight, staying awake, being exposed to light, and being active will interfere with your effort to beat jet lag.

15.

FIFTH MORNING AT DESTINATION: Arise at the time that will be customary during your stay at your destination. Avoid sleeping late. Being active and exposed to bright light in the morning will help you lock in to local time.

TEN TIME ZONES EAST

For example:
From Japan to the U.S. East Coast

1.

Board plane for take-off.

2.

After 10 P.M. in your original time zone, being exposed to light will interfere with your effort to beat jet lag. Therefore, wherever you are at 10 P.M. in your original time zone, put on the dark glasses. If you expect to be asleep at 10 P.M., put on the cloth eyemask before going to sleep. When you wake up, be sure to put on the dark glasses when you take off the eyemask. Be careful as you walk with the glasses on. NOTE: Don't wear the dark glasses if the light level is too low for them to be worn safely.

3.

FIRST MORNING EN ROUTE OR AT DESTI-NATION: Whether you are en route to your destination or have finished crossing ten time zones and have arrived at your destination, be sure to continue to wear the dark glasses, be as inactive as possible, and try to sleep, until 4 A.M. in your original time zone (2 P.M. in the time zone of your destination). Until this time, being exposed to light and being active will interfere with your effort to beat jet lag. Be careful as you walk with the glasses on. NOTE: Don't wear the dark glasses if the light level is too low for them to be worn safely.

4.

At 4 A.M. in your original time zone, remove the dark glasses or the eye-mask. After 4 A.M., especially from 4 to 7 A.M., exposure to light and being

active will help you beat jet lag. If possible, maximize your exposure to sunlight during these hours. NOTE: Do not look directly at the sun or a halogen bulb. If you are flying during this period, try to sit next to a window. If you are on the ground, try to be out of doors as much as possible. If indoors, try to stay near a window or in a brightly illuminated room.

You are likely to be tired during the first day at your destination, but this will be due to lack of a full night's sleep rather than to jet lag.

It's best not to nap during the day or evening, so that you can get a full night's sleep at the end of the day. If you wish to nap, do so between 6 and 10 P.M. in the time zone of your destination, and keep your nap as short as possible.

5.

FIRST NIGHT AT DESTINATION: Try to go to bed between 11 and 2 A.M., local time. Avoid the tendency to stay awake past 2 A.M. After 2 A.M., staying awake, being exposed to light, and being active will interfere with your effort to beat jet lag. Before going to bed, close the curtains, put on a cloth eyemask, and have your dark glasses available so that you can put them on in place of the mask when you get out of bed during the night or in the morning.

6.

SECOND MORNING AT DESTINATION:
Sleeping or remaining inactive until noon would be helpful. If you arise before noon, be sure that you replace your eyemask with the dark glasses. Avoiding early morning light by wearing either the eyemask or dark glasses until noon will help you beat jet lag. Be careful as you walk with the glasses on. NOTE: Don't wear the dark glasses if the light level is too low for them to be worn safely.

7.

Be sure that you are awake and active after noon. Also, remove the dark glasses at noon. Being awake, active, and exposed to bright light from noon until 3 P.M. will help you beat jet lag. If possible, maximize your exposure to sunlight during these hours. NOTE: Do not look directly at the sun or a halogen bulb. Try to be out of doors as much as possible. If indoors, try to stay near a window or in a brightly illuminated room.

It's best not to nap during the day or evening, so that you can get a full night's sleep at the end of the day. If you wish to nap, do so between 3 and 9 P.M., and keep your nap as short as possible.

8.

SECOND NIGHT AT DESTINATION: Try to go to bed before midnight. Avoid the tendency to stay awake past midnight. After midnight, staying awake, being exposed to light, and being active will interfere with your effort to beat jet lag. Before going to bed, close the curtains, put on a cloth eyemask, and have your dark glasses available so that you can put them on in place of the mask when you get out of bed during the night or in the morning.

9.

THIRD MORNING AT DESTINATION: Sleeping or remaining inactive until 10 A.M. would be helpful. If you arise before 10 A.M., be sure that you replace your eyemask with the dark glasses. Avoiding early morning light by wearing either the eyemask or dark glasses until 10 A.M. will help you beat jet lag. Be careful as you walk with the glasses on. NOTE: Don't wear the dark glasses if the light level is too low for them to be worn safely.

10.

Be sure that you are awake and active after 10 A.M. Also, remove the dark glasses at 10 A.M. Being awake, active, and exposed to bright light from 10 A.M. until 1 P.M. will help you beat jet lag. If possible, maximize your exposure to sunlight. NOTE: Do not look directly at the sun or a halogen bulb. Try to be out of doors as much as possible. If indoors, try to stay near a window or in a brightly illuminated room.

It's best not to nap during the day or evening, so that you can get a

full night's sleep at the end of the day. If you wish to nap, do so between 1 and 9 P.M., and keep your nap as short as possible.

II.

THIRD NIGHT AT DESTINATION: Try to go to bed before midnight. After midnight, staying awake, being exposed to light, and being active will interfere with your effort to beat jet lag. If you plan to arise earlier than 8 A.M., then before going to bed, close the curtains, put on a cloth eyemask, and have your dark glasses available so that you can put them on in place of the mask when you get out of bed during the night or in the morning.

I2.

FOURTH MORNING AT DESTINATION: Sleeping or remaining inactive until 8 A.M. would be helpful. If you arise before 8 A.M., be sure that you replace your eyemask with the dark glasses. Avoiding early morning light by wearing either the eyemask or dark glasses until 8 A.M. will help you beat jet lag. Be careful as you walk with the glasses on. NOTE: Don't wear the dark glasses if the light level is too low for them to be worn safely.

I3.

Be sure that you are awake and active after 8 A.M. Also, remove the dark glasses at 8 A.M. Being awake, active, and exposed to bright light from 8 until 11 A.M. will help you beat jet lag. If possible, maximize your exposure to sunlight during these hours. NOTE: Do not look directly at the sun or a halogen bulb. Try to be out of doors as much as possible. If indoors, try to stay near a window or in a brightly illuminated room.

It's best not to nap during the day or evening, so that you can get a full night's sleep at the end of the day. If you wish to nap, do so between 10 A.M. and 9 P.M., and keep your nap as short as possible.

14.

FIFTH NIGHT AT DESTINATION: Try to go to bed before midnight. After midnight, staying awake, being exposed to light, and being active will interfere with your effort to beat jet lag.

15.

SIXTH MORNING AT DESTINATION: Arise at the time that will be customary during your stay at your destination. Avoid sleeping late. Being active and exposed to bright light in the morning will help you lock in to local time.

ELEVEN TIME ZONES EAST

For example:
From Hong Kong to the U.S. East Coast

I.

Board plane for take-off.

2.

After 10 P.M. in your original time zone, being exposed to light will interfere with your effort to beat jet lag. Therefore, wherever you are at 10 P.M. in your original time zone, put on the dark glasses. If you expect to be asleep at 10 P.M., put on the cloth eyemask before going to sleep. When you wake up, be sure to put on the dark glasses when you take off the eyemask. Be careful as you walk with the glasses on. NOTE: Don't wear the dark glasses if the light level is too low for them to be worn safely.

3.

FIRST MORNING EN ROUTE OR AT DESTINATION: Whether you are en route to your destination or have finished crossing eleven time zones and have arrived at your destination, be sure to continue to wear the dark glasses, be as inactive as possible, and try to sleep until 4 A.M. in your original time zone (3 P.M. in the time zone of your destination). Until this time, being exposed to light and being active will interfere with your effort to beat jet lag. Be careful as you walk with the glasses on. NOTE: Don't wear the dark glasses if the light level is too low for them to be worn safely.

4.

At 4 A.M. in your original time zone, remove the dark glasses or the eyemask. After 4 A.M., especially from 4 to 7 A.M., exposure to light and being active will help you beat jet lag. If possible, maximize your exposure to sunlight during these hours. NOTE: Do not look directly at the sun or a halogen bulb. If you are flying during this period, try to sit next to a window. If you are on the ground, try to be out of doors as much as possible. If indoors, try to stay near a window or in a brightly illuminated room.

You are likely to be tired during the first day at your destination, but this will be due to lack of a full night's sleep rather than to jet lag.

It's best not to nap during the day or evening, so that you can get a full night's sleep at the end of the day. If you wish to nap, do so between 7 and 11 P.M. in the time zone of your destination, and keep your nap as short as possible.

5.

FIRST NIGHT AT DESTINATION: Try to go to bed between midnight and 4 A.M., local time. Avoid the tendency to stay awake past 4 A.M. After 4 A.M., staying awake, being exposed to light, and being active will interfere with your effort to beat jet lag. Before going to bed, close the curtains, put on a cloth eyemask, and have your dark glasses available so that you can put them on in place of the mask when you get out of bed during the night or in the morning.

6.

SECOND MORNING AT DESTINATION: Sleeping or remaining inactive until 1 P.M. would be helpful. If you arise before 1 P.M., be sure that you replace your eyemask with the dark glasses. Avoiding early morning light by wearing either the eyemask or the dark glasses until 1 P.M. will help you beat jet lag. Be careful as you walk with the glasses on. NOTE: Don't wear the dark glasses if the light level is too low for them to be worn safely.

7.

Be sure that you are awake and active after 1 P.M. Also, remove the dark glasses at 1 P.M. Being awake, active, and exposed to bright light from 1 until 4 P.M. will help you beat jet lag. If possible, maximize your exposure to sunlight during these hours. NOTE: Do not look directly at the sun or a halogen bulb. Try to be out of doors as much as possible. If indoors, try to stay near a window or in a brightly illuminated room.

It's best not to nap during the day or evening, so that you can get a

full night's sleep at the end of the day. If you wish to nap, do so between 4 and 9 P.M., and keep your nap as short as possible.

8.

SECOND NIGHT AT DESTINATION: Try to go to bed before 2 A.M. Avoid the tendency to stay awake past 2 A.M. After 2 A.M., staying awake, being exposed to light, and being active will interfere with your effort to beat jet lag. Before going to bed, close the curtains, put on a cloth eyemask, and have your dark glasses available so that you can put them on in place of the mask when you get out of bed during the night or in the morning.

9.

THIRD MORNING AT DESTINATION: Sleeping or remaining inactive until 11 A.M. would be helpful. If you arise before 11 A.M., be sure that you replace your eyemask with the dark glasses. Avoiding early morning light by wearing either the eyemask or dark glasses until 11 A.M. will help you beat jet lag. Be careful as you walk with the glasses on. NOTE: Don't wear the dark glasses if the light level is too low for them to be worn safely.

10.

Be sure that you are awake and active after 11 A.M. Also, remove the dark glasses at 11 A.M. Being awake, active, and exposed to bright light from 11 A.M. until 2 P.M. will help you beat jet lag. If possible, maximize your exposure to sunlight during these hours. (Never stare directly at the sun!) Try to be out of doors as much as possible. If indoors, try to stay near a window or in a brightly illuminated room.

It's best not to nap during the day or evening, so that you can get a full night's sleep at the end of the day. If you wish to nap, do so between 2 and 9 P.M., and keep your nap as short as possible.

11.

THIRD NIGHT AT DESTINATION: Try to go to bed before midnight. After midnight, staying awake, being exposed to light, and being active will interfere with your effort to beat jet lag. Before going to bed, close the curtains, put on a cloth eyemask, and have your dark glasses available so that you can put them on in place of the mask when you get out of bed during the night or in the morning.

12.

FOURTH MORNING AT DESTINATION: Sleeping or remaining inactive until 9 A.M. would be helpful. If you arise before 9 A.M., be sure that you replace your eyemask with the dark glasses. Avoiding early morning light by wearing either the eyemask or dark glasses until 9 A.M. will help you beat jet lag. Be careful as you

walk with the glasses on. NOTE: Don't wear the dark glasses if the light level is too low for them to be worn safely.

13.

Be sure that you are awake and active after 9 A.M. Also, remove the dark glasses at 9 A.M. Being awake, active, and exposed to bright light from 9 A.M. until noon will help you beat jet lag. If possible, maximize your exposure to sunlight. NOTE: Do not look directly at the sun or a halogen bulb. Try to be out of doors as much as possible. If indoors, try to stay near a window or in a brightly illuminated room.

It's best not to nap during the day or evening, so that you can get a full night's sleep at the end of the day. If you wish to nap, do so between noon and 9 P.M., and keep your nap as short as possible.

14.

FOURTH NIGHT AT DESTINATION: Try to go to bed before midnight. After midnight, staying awake, being exposed to light, and being active will interfere with your effort to beat jet lag. If you plan to arise earlier than 7 A.M., then before going to bed, close the curtains, put on a cloth eyemask, and have your dark glasses available so that you can put them on in place of the mask when you get out of bed during the night or in the morning.

15.

FIFTH MORNING AT DESTINATION: Sleeping or remaining inactive until 7 A.M. would be helpful. If you arise before 7 A.M., be sure that you replace your eyemask with the dark glasses. Avoiding early morning light by wearing either the eyemask or dark glasses until 7 A.M. will help you beat jet lag. Be careful as you walk with the glasses on. NOTE: Don't wear the dark glasses if the light level is too low for them to be worn safely.

16.

Be sure that you are awake and active after 7 A.M. Also, remove the dark glasses at 7 A.M. Being awake, active, and exposed to bright light from 7 until 10 A.M. will help you beat jet lag. If possible, maximize your exposure to sunlight during these hours. NOTE: Do not look directly at the sun or a halogen bulb. Try to be out of doors as much as possible. If indoors, try to stay near a window or in a brightly illuminated room.

It's best not to nap during the day or evening, so that you can get a full night's sleep at the end of the day. If you wish to nap, do so between 10 A.M. and 9 P.M., and keep your nap as short as possible.

17.

FIFTH NIGHT AT DESTINATION: Try to go to bed before midnight. After midnight, staying awake, being exposed to light, and being active will interfere with your effort to beat jet lag.

18.

SIXTH MORNING AT DESTINATION: Arise at the time that will be customary during your stay at your destination. Avoid sleeping late. Being active and exposed to bright light in the morning will help you lock in to local time.

TWELVE TIME ZONES EAST

For example:
From Thailand to the U.S. East Coast

I.

Board plane for take-off.

2.

After 10 P.M. in your original time zone, being exposed to light will interfere with your effort to beat jet lag. Therefore, wherever you are at 10 P.M. in your original time zone, put on the dark glasses. If you expect to be asleep at 10 P.M., put on the cloth eyemask before going to sleep. When you wake up, be sure to put on the dark glasses when you take off the eyemask. Be careful as you walk with the glasses on. NOTE: Don't wear the dark glasses if the light level is too low for them to be worn safely.

3.

FIRST MORNING EN ROUTE OR AT DESTINATION: Whether you are en route to your destination or have finished crossing twelve time zones and have arrived at your destination, be sure to continue to wear the dark glasses, be as inactive as possible, and try to sleep until 4 A.M. in your original time zone (4 P.M. in the time zone of your destination). Until this hour, being exposed to light and being active will interfere with your effort to beat jet lag. Be careful as you walk with the dark glasses on. NOTE: Don't wear the dark glasses if the light level is too low for them to be worn safely.

4.

At 4 A.M. in your original time zone, remove the dark glasses or eyemask. After 4 A.M., especially from 4 to 7 A.M., exposure to light and being

active will help you beat jet lag. If possible, maximize your exposure to sunlight during these hours. NOTE: Do not look directly at the sun or a halogen bulb. If you are flying during this period, try to sit next to a window. If you are on the ground, try to be out of doors as much as possible. If indoors, try to stay near a window or in a brightly illuminated room.

You are likely to be tired during the first day at your destination, but this will be due to lack of a full night's sleep rather than to jet lag.

It's best not to nap during the day or evening, so that you can get a full night's sleep at the end of the day. If you wish to nap, do so between 8 P.M. and midnight in the time zone of your destination, and keep your nap as short as possible.

5.

FIRST NIGHT AT DESTINATION: Try to go to bed between 2 and 6 A.M., local time. Avoid the tendency to stay awake past 6 A.M. After 6 A.M., staying awake, being exposed to light, and being active will interfere with your effort to beat jet lag. Before going to bed, close the curtains, put on a cloth eyemask, and have your dark glasses available so that you can put them on in place of the mask when you get out of bed during the night or in the morning.

6.

SECOND MORNING AT DESTINATION:
Sleeping or remaining inactive until 2 P.M. would be helpful. If you arise before 2 P.M., be sure that you replace your eyemask with the dark glasses. Avoiding early morning light by wearing either the eyemask or dark glasses and being as inactive as possible until 2 P.M. will help you beat jet lag. Be careful as you walk with the glasses on. NOTE: Don't wear the dark glasses if the light level is too low for them to be worn safely.

7.

Be sure that you are awake and active after 2 P.M. Also, remove the dark glasses at 2 P.M. Being awake, active, and exposed to bright light from 2 until 5 P.M. will help you beat jet lag. If possible, maximize your exposure to sunlight during these hours. NOTE: Do not look directly at the sun or a halogen bulb. Try to be out of doors as much as possible. If indoors, try to stay near a window or in a brightly illuminated room.

It's best not to nap during the day or evening, so that you can get a full night's sleep at the end of the day. If you wish to nap, do so between 5 and 10 P.M., and keep your nap as short as possible.

8.

SECOND NIGHT AT DESTINATION: Try to go to bed before 3 A.M. Avoid the tendency to stay awake past 3 A.M.

After 3 A.M., staying awake, being exposed to light, and being active will interfere with your effort to beat jet lag. Before going to bed, close the curtains, put on a cloth eyemask, and have your dark glasses available so that you can put them on in place of the mask when you get out of bed during the night or in the morning.

9.

THIRD MORNING AT DESTINATION: Sleeping or remaining inactive until noon would be helpful. If you arise before noon, be sure that you replace your eyemask with the dark glasses. Avoiding early morning light by wearing either the eyemask or dark glasses until noon will help you beat jet lag. Be careful as you walk with the glasses on. NOTE: Don't wear the dark glasses if the light level is too low for them to be worn safely.

10.

Be sure that you are awake and active after noon. Also, remove the dark glasses at noon. Being awake, active, and exposed to bright light from noon until 3 P.M. will help you beat jet lag. If possible, maximize your exposure to sunlight during these hours. NOTE: Do not look directly at the sun or a halogen bulb. Try to be out of doors as much as possible. If indoors, try to stay near a window or in a brightly illuminated room.

It's best not to nap during the day or evening, so that you can get a

full night's sleep at the end of the day. If you wish to nap, do so between 3 and 9 P.M., and keep your nap as short as possible.

11.

THIRD NIGHT AT DESTINATION: Try to go to bed before 1 A.M.. After 1 A.M., staying awake, being exposed to light, and being active will interfere with your effort to beat jet lag. Before going to bed, close the curtains, put on a cloth eyemask, and have your dark glasses available so that you can put them on in place of the mask when you get out of bed during the night or in the morning.

12.

FOURTH MORNING AT DESTINATION: Sleeping or remaining inactive until 10 A.M. would be helpful. If you arise before 10 A.M., be sure that you replace your eyemask with the dark glasses. Avoiding early morning light by wearing either the eyemask or dark glasses until 10 A.M. will help you beat jet lag. Be careful as you walk with the glasses on. NOTE: Don't wear the dark glasses if the light level is too low for them to be worn safely.

13.

Be sure that you are awake and active after 10 A.M. Also, remove the dark glasses at 10 A.M. Being awake, active, and exposed to bright light from 10 A.M. until noon will help you beat jet lag. If possible, maximize your exposure to sunlight during these hours. NOTE: Do not look directly at the sun or a halogen bulb. Try to be out of doors as much as possible. If indoors, try to stay near a window or in a brightly illuminated room.

It's best not to nap during the day or evening, so that you can get a full night's sleep at the end of the day. If you wish to nap, do so between 1 and 9 P.M., and keep your nap as short as possible.

14.

FOURTH NIGHT AT DESTINATION: Try to go to bed before midnight. After midnight, staying awake, being exposed to light, and being active will interfere with your effort to beat jet lag. Before going to bed, close the curtains, put on a cloth eyemask, and have your dark glasses available so that you can put them on in place of the mask when you get out of bed during the night or in the morning.

15.

FIFTH MORNING AT DESTINATION: Sleeping or remaining inactive until 8 A.M. would be helpful. If you arise before 8 A.M., be sure that you replace your eyemask with the dark glasses. Avoiding early morning light by wearing either the eyemask or dark glasses until 8 A.M. will help you beat jet lag. Be careful as you walk with the glasses on. NOTE: Don't wear the dark glasses if the light level is too low for them to be worn safely.

16.

Be sure that you are awake and active after 8 A.M. Also, remove the dark glasses at 8 A.M. Being awake, active, and exposed to bright light from 8 until 11 A.M. will help you beat jet lag. If possible, maximize your exposure to sunlight during these hours. NOTE: Do not look directly at the sun or a halogen bulb. Try to be out of doors as much as possible. If indoors, try to stay near a window or in a brightly illuminated room.

It's best not to nap during the day or evening, so that you can get a full night's sleep at the end of the day. If you wish to nap, do so between 11 A.M. and 9 P.M., and keep your nap as short as possible.

17.

FIFTH NIGHT AT DESTINATION: Try to go to bed before midnight. After midnight, staying awake, being exposed to light, and being active will interfere with your effort to beat jet lag.

18.

SIXTH MORNING AT DESTINATION: Arise at the time that will be customary during your stay at your destination. Avoid sleeping late. Being active and exposed to bright light in the morning will help you lock in to local time.

Beating Jet Lag on Flights Westward

THREE TIME ZONES WEST

For example:
From the U.S. East Coast to the U.S. West Coast

1. DAY OR NIGHT OF DEPARTURE: Board plane. If you are leaving before 10 A.M., wear dark glasses until then. Avoiding bright light before 10 A.M. will help you avoid jet lag. NOTE: Don't wear the dark glasses if the light level is too low for them to be worn safely. If you are leaving after 10 A.M., do not wear dark glasses; exposure to light after 10 A.M. can be helpful.

2. After about six hours, the plane has crossed three time zones and lands. If it is still light outside at 9 P.M., local time, exposure to daylight will be helpful. NOTE: Do not look directly at the sun or a halogen bulb.

3.

Because bright light in the late evening will help you beat jet lag, try to arrive at a place where you can be exposed to daylight or bright artificial light by about 9 P.M., local time.

4.

FIRST NIGHT AT DESTINATION: Either walk in the bright light outside or sit near a bright light and glance at it every few minutes between 9 P.M. and midnight, local time. Though you will probably feel drowsy, significant exposure to light during this time period will help you beat jet lag. NOTE: Do not look directly at the sun or a halogen bulb.

5.

Before going to bed, or by 1 A.M. at the latest, put on a cloth eyemask. Have your dark glasses available so that you can put them on in place of the mask should you have to get out of bed in the middle of the night.

6.

FIRST MORNING AT DESTINATION: If you must arise from bed before 6 A.M., be sure that you replace your eyemask with the dark glasses. Avoiding bright light between 1 and 6 A.M. will help you avoid jet lag. Always be careful as you walk with the glasses on. NOTE: Don't wear the dark glasses if the light level is too low for them to be worn safely.

7.

You may remove the eyemask or dark glasses anytime after 6 A.M. Though you may have some slight, residual tiredness from staying up late the night before, your internal clock should be almost completely adjusted to the local time.

8.

SECOND NIGHT AT DESTINATION: Some people adjust more quickly than others. If you are feeling tired on the second night at your destination, you may have a "booster" light treatment by glancing at a bright light every few minutes for one hour anytime between 9 and 11 P.M. NOTE: Do not look directly at the sun or a halogen bulb. This last round of light exposure will help lock your body clock in to the desired time zone.

FOUR TIME ZONES WEST

For example:
From the U.S. Midwest to Hawaii

1. DAY OR NIGHT OF DEPARTURE: Board plane. If you are leaving before 10 A.M., wear dark glasses until then. Avoiding bright light before 10 A.M. will help you avoid jet lag. NOTE: Don't wear the dark glasses if the light level is too low for them to be worn safely. If you are leaving after 10 A.M., do not wear dark glasses; exposure to light after 10 A.M. can be helpful.

2.   After about eight hours, the plane has crossed four time zones and lands. Because of its brightness, exposure to daylight between 6 P.M. local time and sunset can help you beat jet lag. Note: Do not look directly at the sun.

3.   Because bright light in the late evening will help you beat jet lag, try to arrive at a place where you can be exposed to daylight or bright artificial light by about 8 P.M., local time. If you are tired from the long flight, you may take a one-hour nap. Be sure, however, that you are awake again by 8 P.M.

4.

FIRST NIGHT AT DESTINATION: Either walk in the bright light outside or sit near a bright light and glance at it every few minutes between 8 and 11 P.M., local time. NOTE: Do not look directly at the sun or a halogen bulb. Though you might feel tired during this interval, significant exposure to light during this time period will help you beat jet lag.

5.

You may go to bed anytime after 11 P.M. Before going to bed, or by midnight at the latest, put on a cloth eyemask. Have your dark glasses available so that you can put them on in place of the mask should you have to get out of bed in the middle of the night. NOTE: Don't wear the dark glasses if the light level is too low for them to be worn safely.

6.

If you must arise from bed for any reason between midnight and 6 A.M., be sure that you replace your eyemask with the dark glasses. Avoiding bright light before 6 A.M. will help you avoid jet lag. Always be careful as you walk with the glasses on. NOTE: Don't wear the dark glasses if the light level is too low for them to be worn safely. Though you will naturally tend to awaken early, try to stay in bed until 6 A.M.

7.

FIRST MORNING AT DESTINATION: You may remove the eyemask or dark glasses anytime after 6 A.M. Though you may have some slight, residual tiredness from staying up late the night before, your internal clock is well on its way to being adjusted to the local time.

8.

SECOND NIGHT AT DESTINATION: Avoid going to sleep early on the second night at your destination. Sit near a bright light and glance at it every few minutes between 8 and 10 P.M. This last round of light exposure will help lock your body clock in to the desired time zone.

FIVE TIME ZONES WEST

For example:
From England to the U.S. East Coast

I.

DAY OR NIGHT OF DEPARTURE: Board plane. If you are leaving before 10 A.M., wear dark glasses until then. Avoiding bright light before 10 A.M. will help you avoid jet lag. NOTE: Don't wear the dark glasses if the light level is too low for them to be worn safely. If you are leaving after 10 A.M., do not wear dark glasses; exposure to light after 10 A.M. can be helpful.

2.

After about eight hours, the plane has crossed five time zones and lands. Because of its brightness, exposure to daylight between 5 P.M. local time and sunset can help you beat jet lag. Outdoor physical activity or walks are particularly good at this time. NOTE: Do not look directly at the sun or a halogen bulb.

3.

Because bright light in the late evening will help you beat jet lag, try to arrive at a place where you can be exposed to daylight or bright artificial light by about 7 P.M., local time. If you are tired from the long flight, you may take a one-hour nap. Be sure, however, that you are awake again by 7 P.M.

4.

FIRST NIGHT AT DESTINATION: Either walk in the bright light outside or sit near a bright light and glance at it every few minutes between 7 and 10 P.M., local time. NOTE: Do not look directly at the sun or a halogen bulb. Though you will probably prefer to sleep during this interval, significant exposure to light during this time period will help you beat jet lag.

5.

It is very important to avoid bright light after 11 P.M. If possible, go to bed. If that is impossible, wear your dark glasses after 11 P.M. until you can get to bed. NOTE: Don't wear the dark glasses if the light level is too low for them to be worn safely. Before going to bed, put on a cloth eyemask. Have your dark glasses available so that you can put them on in place of the mask should you have to get out of bed in the middle of the night.

6.

If you must arise from bed for any reason between 11 P.M. and 5 A.M., be sure that you replace your eyemask with the dark glasses. Avoiding bright light before 5 A.M. will help you avoid jet lag. Always be careful as you walk with the glasses on. NOTE: Don't wear the dark glasses if the light level is too low for them to be worn safely. Though you will naturally tend to awaken early, try to stay in bed until 5 A.M.

7.

FIRST MORNING AT DESTINATION: You may remove the eyemask or dark glasses anytime after 5 A.M. Though you may have some slight, residual tiredness from staying up late the night before, your internal clock is well on its way to being adjusted to the local time.

8.

SECOND NIGHT AT DESTINATION: Avoid going to sleep early on the second night at your destination. Sit near a bright light and glance at it every few minutes between 8 and 10 P.M. This last round of light exposure will help lock your body clock in to the desired time zone.

SIX TIME ZONES WEST

For example:
From Europe to the U.S. East Coast

I.

Board plane. If you are leaving before 10 A.M., wear dark glasses until then. Avoiding bright light before 10 A.M. will help you avoid jet lag. NOTE: Don't wear the dark glasses if the light level is too low for them to be worn safely. If you are leaving after 10 A.M., do not wear dark glasses; exposure to light after 10 A.M. can be helpful.

2.

After about nine hours, the plane has crossed six time zones and lands. Because of its brightness, exposure to daylight between 5 and 9 P.M., local time, can help you beat jet lag. Outdoor physical activity or walks are particularly good at this time. Note: Do not look directly at the sun.

3.

Because bright light in the late evening will help you beat jet lag, try to arrive at a place where you can be exposed to daylight or bright artificial light by about 6 P.M., local time. If you are tired from the long flight, you may take a one-hour nap. Be sure, however, that you are awake again by 6 P.M.

4.

FIRST NIGHT AT DESTINATION: Either walk in the bright light outside or sit near a bright light and glance at it every few minutes between 6 and 9 P.M., local time. NOTE: Do not look directly at the sun or a halogen bulb. Though you will probably prefer to sleep during this interval, significant exposure to light during this time period will help you beat jet lag.

5.

It is very important to avoid bright light after 10 P.M. If possible, go to bed. If that is impossible, wear your dark glasses after 10 P.M. until you can get to bed. NOTE: Don't wear the dark glasses if the light level is too low for them to be worn safely. Before going to bed, put on a cloth eyemask. Have your dark glasses available so that you can put them on in place of the mask should you have to get out of bed in the middle of the night.

6.

If you must arise from bed for any reason between 10 P.M. and 4 A.M., be sure that you replace your eyemask with the dark glasses. Avoiding bright light before 4 A.M. will help you avoid jet lag. Always be careful as you walk with the glasses on. NOTE: Don't wear the dark glasses if the light level is too low for them to be worn safely. Though you will naturally tend to awaken early, try to stay in bed until 5 A.M.

7.

FIRST MORNING AT DESTINATION: You may remove the eyemask or dark glasses anytime after 4 A.M. Though you may have some residual tiredness from staying up late the night before, your internal clock is well on its way to being adjusted to the local time.

8.

Though you may take a midday nap, if you feel you need one, avoid going to sleep early on the second night at your destination. Either walk in the bright light outside or sit near a bright light and glance at it every few minutes between 6 and 9 P.M. NOTE: Do not look directly at the sun or a halogen bulb.

9.

SECOND NIGHT AT DESTINATION: Wear the eyemask while you sleep and keep it on until at least 6 A.M. This last round of light deprivation will help lock your body clock in to the desired time zone.

SEVEN TIME ZONES WEST

For example:
From Europe to the U.S. Midwest

I.

Board plane. If you are leaving before 10 A.M., wear dark glasses until then. Avoiding bright light before 10 A.M. will help you avoid jet lag. NOTE: Don't wear the dark glasses if the light level is too low for them to be worn safely. If you are leaving after 10 A.M., do not wear dark glasses; exposure to light after 10 A.M. can be helpful.

2.

After about ten hours, the plane has crossed seven time zones and lands. Because of its brightness, exposure to daylight between 4 and 8 P.M., local time, can help you beat jet lag. Note: Do not look directly at the sun.

3.

If you are tired from the long flight, you may take a one-hour nap. Be sure, however, that you are awake again by 5 P.M.

4.

FIRST NIGHT AT DESTINATION: Either walk in the bright light outside or sit near a bright light and glance at it every few minutes between 5 and 8 P.M., local time. NOTE: Do not look directly at the sun or a halogen bulb. Though you will probably prefer to sleep during this interval, significant exposure to light during this time period will help you beat jet lag.

5.

It is very important to avoid bright light after 9 P.M. If possible, go to bed. If that is impossible, wear your dark glasses after 9 P.M. until you can get to bed. NOTE: Don't wear the dark glasses if the light level is too low for them to be worn safely. Before going to bed, put on a cloth eyemask. Have your dark glasses available so that you can put them on in place of the mask should you have to get out of bed in the middle of the night.

6.

If you must arise from bed for any reason between 9 P.M. and 4 A.M., be sure that you replace your eyemask with the dark glasses. You are avoiding the harmful light of your first night in the West by wearing either the eyemask or dark glasses until at least 4 A.M. Always be careful as you walk with the glasses on. NOTE: Don't wear the dark glasses if the light level is too low for them to be worn safely. Though you will naturally want to awaken early, resist the tendency to arise before 4 A.M. If you can stay in bed later, try doing so.

7.

FIRST MORNING AT DESTINATION: You may remove the eyemask or dark glasses anytime after 4 A.M. Though you may have residual tiredness from staying up late the night before, your internal clock is well on its way to being adjusted to the local time.

8.

Though you may take a midday nap, if you feel you need one, avoid the tendency to go to sleep early on your second evening at your destination.

Instead, either walk in the bright light outside or sit near a bright light and glance at it every few minutes between 6 and 8 P.M. NOTE: Do not look directly at the sun or a halogen bulb.

9.

SECOND NIGHT AT YOUR DESTINATION: Wear the eyemask while you sleep and keep it on until at least 6 A.M. This last round of light deprivation will help lock your body clock in to the desired time zone.

EIGHT TIME ZONES WEST

For example:
From England to the U.S. West Coast

1.

Board plane. If you are leaving before 10 A.M., wear dark glasses until then. Avoiding bright light before 10 A.M. will help you avoid jet lag. NOTE: Don't wear the dark glasses if the light level is too low for them to be worn safely. If you are leaving after

10 A.M., do not wear dark glasses; exposure to light after 10 A.M. can be helpful.

2.

After about twelve hours, the plane has crossed eight time zones and lands. Because of its brightness, exposure to daylight between 2 and 7 P.M., local time, can help you beat jet lag. Note: Do not look directly at the sun. If you are on board a connecting flight that will arrive after 2 P.M., destination time, be sure to request a window seat and glance outside every few minutes after 2 P.M., destination time.

3.

Any exposure to bright light after 2 P.M., local time, will help you beat jet lag. Outdoor physical activity or walks are particularly good at this time.

Either walk in the bright light outside or sit near a bright light and glance at it every few minutes until 7 P.M. NOTE: Do not look directly at the sun or a halogen bulb. Though you will probably prefer to sleep during this interval, significant exposure to light during this time period will help you beat jet lag.

4.

FIRST NIGHT AT DESTINATION: It is very important to avoid bright light after 8 P.M. If possible, go to bed. If that is impossible, wear your dark glasses after 8 P.M. until you can get to bed. Before going to bed, put on a cloth eyemask. NOTE: Don't wear the dark glasses if the light level is too low for them to be worn safely. Have your dark glasses available so that you can put them on in place of the mask should you have to get out of bed in the middle of the night.

5.

If you must arise from bed for any reason between 8 P.M. and 3 A.M., be sure that you replace your eyemask with the dark glasses. Avoiding bright light before 3 A.M. will help you avoid jet lag. Always be careful as you walk with the glasses on. NOTE: Don't wear the dark glasses if the light level is too low for them to be worn safely. Though you will be likely to awaken early, resist the tendency to arise before 3 A.M. If you can stay in bed later, try doing so.

6.

FIRST MORNING AT DESTINATION: You may remove the eyemask or dark glasses anytime after 3 A.M. Though you may have residual tiredness from the long trip the day before, your internal clock is well on its way to being adjusted to the local time.

7.

Though you may take a midday nap, if you feel you need one, avoid the tendency to go to sleep early on your second evening at your destination. Instead, walk in bright light or sit near a bright light and glance at it every few minutes between 6 and 9 P.M. NOTE: Do not look directly at the sun or a halogen bulb.

8.

SECOND NIGHT AT DESTINATION: You should go to bed by midnight. Before going to bed, put on a cloth eyemask. Have your dark glasses available so that you can put them on in place of the mask should you have to get out of bed in the middle of the night. NOTE: Don't wear the dark glasses if the light level is too low for them to be worn safely.

9.

If you must arise from bed for any reason between midnight and 7 A.M., be sure that you replace your eyemask with the dark glasses. NOTE: Don't wear the dark glasses if the light level is too low for them to be worn safely. Avoiding bright light before 7 A.M. will help you avoid jet lag. Always be careful as you walk with the glasses on. Though you will be likely to awaken early, resist the tendency to arise before 7 A.M. If you can stay in bed later, try doing so.

10.

THIRD NIGHT AT DESTINATION: If you have not fully adjusted to local time by your third day at your destination, you may need an optional booster of light exposure. Sit near a bright light and glance at it every few minutes between 9 and 11 P.M. NOTE: Do not look directly at the sun or a halogen bulb. This last round of light will help lock your body clock in to the desired time zone.

NINE TIME ZONES WEST

For example:
From Western Europe to the U.S. West Coast

1.

Do not adjust your watch until instructed to do so! Board plane. If you are leaving before 10 A.M., wear dark glasses until then. Avoiding bright light before 10 A.M. will help you avoid jet lag. NOTE: Don't wear the dark glasses if the light level is too low for them to be worn safely. If you are leaving after 10 A.M., do not wear dark glasses; exposure to light later in the day can be helpful.

2.

After about ten hours, the plane has reached a connecting airport for a stopover. It does not matter how much or how little light you are exposed to at this time.

3.

Be sure to ask for a window seat for the final leg of your journey. It is fine to nap on this flight before midnight. After that, be sure to be awake and frequently glance out the window if it is light outside. NOTE: Do not look directly at the sun or a halogen bulb.

4.

After midnight you should adjust your watch to the time at your destination. (For example, midnight becomes 3 P.M.)

5.

After a few more hours of flight, your plane lands. Beginning at 4 P.M., local time, exposure to sunlight or other bright lights will help you beat jet lag.

6.

Exposure to bright light between 1 P.M. and 6 P.M., local time, is important. Outdoor physical activity or walks are particularly good at this time. If the weather prevents you from being outside, try to find an indoor location where you may be exposed to bright light. NOTE: Do not look directly at the sun or a halogen bulb. Though you will probably prefer to sleep during this interval, significant exposure to light during this time period will help you beat jet lag.

7.

FIRST NIGHT AT DESTINATION: It is very important to avoid bright light after 7 P.M., local time. If possible, go to bed. If that is impossible, wear your dark glasses after 7 P.M. until you can get to bed. NOTE: Don't wear the dark glasses if the light level is too low for them to be worn safely. Before going to bed, put on a cloth eyemask. Have your dark glasses available so that you can put them on in place of the mask should you have to get out of bed in the middle of the night.

8.

If you must arise from bed for any reason between 7 P.M. and 2 A.M., be sure that you replace your eyemask with the dark glasses. Avoiding bright light before 2 A.M. will help you avoid jet lag. Always be careful as you walk with the glasses on. NOTE: Don't wear the dark glasses if the light level is too low for them to be worn safely. Though you will naturally want to awaken early, resist the tendency to arise before 2 A.M. If you can stay in bed later, try doing so.

9.

FIRST MORNING AT DESTINATION: You may remove the eyemask or dark glasses anytime after 2 A.M. If you wish to read a book or prepare for your day's activities after this hour, your body clock will not be affected. If you wish to sleep again later that night, that is also fine. Though you may have residual tiredness from the long trip the day before, your internal clock is well on its way to being adjusted to the local time.

10.

Though you may take a midday nap, if you feel you need one, avoid the tendency to go to sleep early on your second evening at your destination. Instead, walk in bright light or sit near a bright light and glance at it every few minutes between 5 P.M. and 8 P.M. NOTE: Do not look directly at the sun or a halogen bulb.

11.

SECOND NIGHT AT DESTINATION: If possible, you should go to bed by 10 P.M. Before going to bed, put on a cloth eyemask. Have your dark glasses available so that you can put them on in place of the mask should you have to get out of bed in the middle of the night. NOTE: Don't wear the dark glasses if the light level is too low for them to be worn safely.

12.

If you must arise from bed for any reason between 10 P.M. and 6 A.M., be sure that you replace your eyemask with the dark glasses. Avoiding bright light before 6 A.M. will help you avoid jet lag. Always be careful as you walk with the glasses on. NOTE: Don't wear the dark glasses if the light level is too low for them to be worn safely. Though you will be likely to awaken early, resist the tendency to arise before 6 A.M. If you can stay in bed later, try doing so.

13.

THIRD NIGHT AT DESTINATION: Your flight has been a difficult one. If you feel as though you have not fully adjusted to local time by your third day at your destination, you may need an optional booster of light exposure. Either walk in the bright light outside or sit near a bright light and glance at it every few minutes between 8 and 10 P.M. NOTE: Do not look directly at the sun or a halogen bulb. This last round of light will help lock your body clock in to the desired time zone.

TEN TIME ZONES WEST

For example:
From the U.S. East Coast to Japan

1.

Do not adjust your watch until instructed to do so! Board plane. If you are leaving before 10 A.M., wear dark glasses until then. Avoiding bright light before 10 A.M. will help you avoid jet lag. NOTE: Don't wear the dark glasses if the light level is too low for them to be worn safely. If you are leaving after 10 A.M., do not wear dark glasses; exposure to light later in the day can be helpful.

2.

After a few hours, the plane has reached your connecting airport for a stopover or change of planes.

3.

Be sure to ask for a window seat for the final leg of your journey. It is fine to nap on this flight before midnight. After that be sure to be awake and frequently glance out the window if it is light outside. NOTE: Do not look directly at the sun or a halogen bulb.

4.

After midnight you should adjust your watch to the time at your destination. (For example, midnight becomes 2 P.M.)

5.

After several more hours of flight, your plane lands. Between 2 and 5 P.M. (on your reset watch) exposure to sunlight or other bright lights will help you beat jet lag. NOTE: Do not look directly at the sun or a halogen bulb.

6.

Because bright light in the evening must be avoided to beat jet lag, try to arrive at your destination by about 5 P.M., local time. In any case, put your dark glasses on between 5 and 6 P.M. Always be careful as you walk with the glasses on. NOTE: Don't wear the dark glasses if the light level is too low for them to be worn safely.

7.

FIRST NIGHT AT DESTINATION: It is very important to avoid bright light after 6 P.M. If possible, go to bed. If that is impossible, wear your dark glasses after 6 P.M. until you can get to bed. NOTE: Don't wear the dark glasses if the light level is too low for them to be worn safely. Before going to bed, put on a cloth eyemask. Have your dark glasses available so that you can put them on in place of the mask should you have to get out of bed in the middle of the night. Exposure to light after 6 P.M. will make your jet lag worse.

8.

If you must arise from bed for any reason between 6 P.M. and 1 A.M., be sure that you replace your eyemask with dark glasses. Avoiding bright light before 1 A.M. will help you avoid jet lag. Always be careful as you walk with the glasses on. NOTE: Don't wear the dark glasses if the light level is too low for them to be worn safely. Though you will naturally want to awaken early, resist the tendency to arise before 1 A.M. If you can stay in bed later, try doing so.

9.

FIRST MORNING AT DESTINATION: You may remove the eyemask or dark glasses anytime after 1 A.M. If you wish to read a book or prepare for your day's activities after this hour, your body clock should not be affected. If you wish to sleep again later that night, that is also fine. Though you may have residual tiredness from the long trip the day before, your internal clock is well on its way to being adjusted to the local time.

10.

Though you may take a midday nap, if you feel you need one, avoid the tendency to go to sleep early on your second evening at your destination. Instead, walk in bright light or sit near a bright light and glance at it every few minutes between 3 and 7 P.M. NOTE: Do not look directly at the sun or a halogen bulb.

11.

SECOND NIGHT AT DESTINATION: If possible, you should go to bed by 9 P.M. Before going to bed, put on a cloth eyemask and have your dark glasses available so that you can put them on in place of the mask should you have to get out of bed in the middle of the night. NOTE: Don't wear the dark glasses if the light level is too low for them to be worn safely.

12.

SECOND NIGHT AT DESTINATION: If you must arise from bed for any reason between 9 P.M. and 5 A.M., be sure that you replace your eyemask with the dark glasses. Avoiding bright light before 5 A.M. will help you avoid jet lag. Always be careful as you walk with the glasses on. NOTE: Don't wear the dark glasses if the light level is too low for them to be worn safely. Though you will be likely to awaken early, resist the tendency to arise before 5 A.M. If you can stay in bed later, try doing so.

13.

THIRD NIGHT AT DESTINATION: Your flight has been a difficult one. If you feel as though you have not fully adjusted to local time by your third day at your destination, you may need an optional booster of light exposure. Sit near a bright light and glance at it every few minutes between 7 and 9 P.M. NOTE: Do not look directly at the sun or a halogen bulb. This last round of light will help lock your body clock in to the desired time zone.

ELEVEN TIME ZONES WEST

For example:
From the U.S. East Coast to Hong Kong

1.

Do not adjust your watch until instructed to do so! Board plane. If you are leaving before 10 P.M., wear dark glasses until then. Avoiding bright light before 10 A.M. will help you avoid jet lag. NOTE: Don't wear the dark glasses if the light level is too low for them to be worn safely. If you are leaving after 10 A.M., do not wear dark glasses; exposure to light later in the day can be helpful.

2.

After a number of hours, the plane has reached your connecting airport for a stopover or change of planes.

3.

If possible, select a window seat for the final leg of your journey. Before 9 P.M. on your watch (which is still set to your original time zone) it is fine to nap on this flight. Between 9 P.M. and 3 A.M. (especially between midnight and 3 A.M.), however, it is important that you are awake and that you frequently glance out the window. NOTE: Do not look directly at the sun or a halogen bulb. This light exposure will help your body clock adjust to the new time zone.

4.

After 3 A.M. you should adjust your watch to the time at your destination. (For example, 3 A.M. becomes 4 P.M.)

5.

Avoiding bright light after 5 P.M. (on your reset watch) will help you beat jet lag. If you can fall asleep after 5 P.M., that's good. Before trying to sleep, put on a cloth eyemask. Have your dark glasses available so that you can put them on in place of the mask as soon as you awake. NOTE: Don't wear the dark glasses if the light level is too low for them to be worn safely.

6.

After several more hours of flight, your plane lands. You are avoiding light by wearing the dark glasses full-time as you disembark. Always be careful as you walk with the glasses on. Because bright light in the evening must be avoided to beat jet lag, keep your dark glasses on after 5 P.M. in your destination time zone. NOTE: Don't wear the dark glasses if the light level is too low for them to be worn safely.

7.

FIRST NIGHT AT DESTINATION: It is very important to avoid bright light after 5 P.M., local time. If possible, go to bed. If that is impossible, wear your dark glasses after 5 P.M. until you can get to bed. NOTE: Don't wear the dark glasses if the light level is too low for them to be worn safely. Before going to bed, put on a cloth eyemask. Have your dark glasses available so that you can put them on in place of the mask should you have to get out of bed in the middle of the night.

8.

If you must be out of bed for any reason between 5 P.M. and midnight, be sure that you replace your eyemask with the dark glasses. Avoiding bright light before midnight will help you avoid jet lag. Always be careful as you walk with the glasses on. NOTE: Don't wear the dark glasses if the light level is too low for them to be worn safely. Though you will naturally want to awaken early, resist the tendency to arise before midnight. If you can stay in bed later, try doing so.

9.

You may remove the eyemask or dark glasses anytime after midnight. If you wish to read a book or prepare for the next day's activities after this hour, your body clock should not be affected. If you wish to sleep again later that night, that is good. Though you will likely have residual tiredness from the long trip during your first day, your internal clock is well on its way to being adjusted to the local time.

10.

FIRST MORNING AT DESTINATION: Though you may take a midmorning nap if you feel you need one, avoid the tendency to sleep in the afternoon. Instead, walk in bright light or sit near a bright light and glance at it every few minutes between 3 and 6 P.M. NOTE: Do not look directly at the sun or a halogen bulb.

11.

SECOND NIGHT AT DESTINATION: If possible, you should go to bed by 8 P.M. Before going to bed, put on a cloth eyemask. Have your dark glasses available so that you can put them on in place of the mask should you have to get out of bed in the middle of the night. NOTE: Don't wear the dark glasses if the light level is too low for them to be worn safely.

12.

SECOND NIGHT AT DESTINATION: If you must arise from bed for any reason between 8 P.M. and 4 A.M., be sure that you replace your eyemask with the dark glasses. Avoiding bright light before 4 A.M. will help you avoid jet lag. Always be careful as you walk with the glasses on. NOTE: Don't wear the dark glasses if the light level is too low for them to be worn safely. Though you will be likely to awaken early, resist the tendency to arise before 4 A.M. If you can stay in bed later, try doing so.

13.

THIRD NIGHT AT DESTINATION: Your flight has been a difficult one. If you feel as though you have not fully adjusted to local time by your third day at your destination, you may need an optional booster of light exposure. Sit near a bright light and glance at it every few minutes between 6 and 8 P.M. NOTE: Do not look directly at the sun or a halogen bulb. This last round of light exposure will help lock your body clock in to the desired time zone. You will have accomplished in less than three days what would normally take your body a week and a half!

TWELVE TIME ZONES WEST

For example:
From the U.S. East Coast to Thailand

1.

Do not adjust your watch until instructed to do so! Board plane. If you are leaving before 10 A.M., wear dark glasses until then. Avoiding bright light before 10 A.M. will help you avoid jet lag. NOTE: Don't wear the dark glasses if the light level is too low for them to be worn safely. If you are leaving after 10 A.M., do not wear dark glasses; exposure to light later in the day can be helpful.

2.

After a number of hours, the plane has reached your connecting airport for a stopover or change of planes.

3.

If possible, select a window seat for the final leg of your journey. Before 9 P.M. on your watch (which is still set to your original time zone) it is fine to nap on this flight. Between 9 P.M. and 3 A.M. (especially between midnight and 3 A.M.), however, it is important that you are awake and that you frequently glance out the window. This light exposure will help your body clock adjust to the new time zone. NOTE: Do not look directly at the sun or a halogen bulb.

4.

After 3 A.M. you should adjust your watch to the time at your destination. (For example, 3 A.M. becomes 3 P.M.)

5.

Avoiding bright light after 4 P.M. (on your reset watch) will help you beat jet lag. If you can fall asleep after 4 P.M., that's good. Before trying to sleep, put on a cloth eyemask. Have your dark glasses available so that you can put them on in place of the mask as soon as you awaken. NOTE: Don't wear the dark glasses if the light level is too low for them to be worn safely.

6.

After several more hours of flight, your plane lands. You are avoiding light by wearing the dark glasses full-time as you disembark. Always be careful as you walk with the glasses on. Because bright light in the late afternoon and evening must be avoided to beat jet lag, keep your dark glasses on after 4 P.M. in your destination time zone.

7.

FIRST EVENING AT DESTINATION: It is very important to avoid bright light after 4 P.M., local time. If possible, go to bed. If that is impossible, wear your dark glasses after 4 P.M. until you can get to bed. NOTE: Don't wear the dark glasses if the light level is too low for them to be worn safely. Before going to bed, put on a cloth eyemask. Have your dark glasses available so that you can put them on in place of the mask should you have to get out of bed in the middle of the night. NOTE: Don't wear the dark glasses if the light level is too low for them to be worn safely.

8.

If you must be out of bed for any reason between 4 and 11 P.M., be sure that you replace your eyemask with the dark glasses. Avoiding bright light before 11 P.M. will help you avoid jet lag. Always be careful as you walk with the glasses on. NOTE: Don't wear the dark glasses if the light level is too low for them to be worn safely. Though you will naturally want to awaken early, resist the tendency to arise before 11 P.M. If you can stay in bed later, try doing so.

9.

You may remove the eyemask or dark glasses anytime after 11 P.M. If you wish to read a book or prepare for the next day's activities after this hour your body clock will not be affected. If you wish to sleep again later that night, that is good. Though you will likely have residual tiredness from the long trip during your first day, your internal clock is well on its way to being adjusted to the local time.

10.

FIRST MORNING AT DESTINATION: Though you may take a midmorning nap, if you feel you need one, avoid the tendency to sleep in the afternoon. Instead, walk in bright light or sit near a bright light and glance at it every few minutes between 2 and 5 P.M. NOTE: Do not look directly at the sun or a halogen bulb.

11.

SECOND EVENING AT DESTINATION: If possible, you should go to bed by 7 P.M. Before going to bed, put on a cloth eyemask. Have your dark glasses available so that you can put them on in place of the mask should you have to get out of bed in the middle of the night. NOTE: Don't wear the dark glasses if the light level is too low for them to be worn safely.

12.

SECOND NIGHT AT DESTINATION: If you must arise from bed for any reason between 7 P.M. and 3 A.M., be sure that you replace your eyemask with the dark glasses. Avoiding bright light before 3 A.M. will help you avoid jet lag. Always be careful as you walk with the glasses on. NOTE: Don't wear the dark glasses if the light level is too low for them to be worn safely. Though you will be likely to awaken early, resist the tendency to arise before 3 A.M. If you can stay in bed later, try doing so.

13.

THIRD EVENING AT DESTINATION: Your flight has been a difficult one. If you feel as though you have not fully adjusted to local time by the third day at your destination, you may need an optional booster of light exposure. Either walk in the bright light outside or sit near a bright light and glance at it every few minutes between 5 and 7 P.M. NOTE: Do not look directly at the sun or a halogen bulb. This last round of light exposure will help lock your body clock in to the desired time zone. You will have accomplished in less than three days what would normally take your body a week and a half!

THIRTEEN TIME ZONES WEST

For example:
From Hawaii to Western Europe

1.

Do not adjust your watch until instructed to do so! Board plane. If you are leaving before 10 A.M., wear dark glasses until then. Avoiding bright light before 10 A.M. will help you avoid jet lag. NOTE: Don't wear the dark glasses if the light level is too low for them to be worn safely. If you are leaving after 10 A.M., do not wear dark glasses; exposure to light later in the day can be helpful.

2.

After a number of hours, the plane has reached your connecting airport for a stopover or change of planes.

3.

If possible, select a window seat for the final leg of your journey. Before 9 P.M. on your watch (which is still set to your original time zone) it is fine to nap on this flight. Between 9 P.M. and 3 A.M. (especially between midnight and 3 A.M.) it is important that you are awake and that you frequently glance out the window. This light exposure will help your body clock adjust to the new time zone. NOTE: Do not look directly at the sun or a halogen bulb.

4.

After 3 A.M. you should adjust your watch to the time at your destination. (For example, 3 A.M. becomes 2 P.M.)

5.

Avoiding bright light after 3 P.M. (on your reset watch) will help you beat jet lag. If you can fall asleep after 3 P.M., that's good. Before trying to sleep, put on a cloth eyemask. Have your dark glasses available so that you can put them on in place of the mask as soon as you awake. NOTE: Don't wear the dark glasses if the light level is too low for them to be worn safely.

6.

After several more hours of flight, your plane lands. You are avoiding light by wearing the dark glasses full-time as you disembark. Always be careful as you walk with the glasses on. NOTE: Don't wear the dark glasses if the light level is too low for them to be worn safely. Because bright light in the evening must be avoided to beat jet lag, keep your dark glasses on after 3 P.M. in your destination time zone.

7.

FIRST AFTERNOON AT DESTINATION: It is very important to avoid bright light after 3 P.M., local time. If possible, go to bed. If that is impossible, wear your dark glasses after 3 P.M. until you can get to bed. NOTE: Don't wear the dark glasses if the light level is too low for them to be worn safely. Before going to bed, put on a cloth eyemask. Have your dark glasses available so that you can put them on in place of the mask should you have to get out of bed in the middle of the night.

8.

If you must be out of bed for any reason between 3 and 10 P.M., local time, be sure that you replace your eyemask with the dark glasses. Avoiding bright light before 10 P.M. will help you avoid jet lag. Always be careful as you walk with the glasses on. NOTE: Don't wear the dark glasses if the light level is too low for them to be worn safely. Though you will naturally want to awaken early, resist the tendency to arise before 10 P.M. If you can stay in bed later, try doing so.

9.

FIRST NIGHT AT DESTINATION: You may remove the eyemask or dark glasses anytime after 10 P.M. If you wish to read a book or prepare for the next day's activities after this hour your body clock should not be affected. If you wish to sleep again later that night, that is good. Though you will likely have residual tiredness from the long trip during your first day, your internal clock is well on its way to being adjusted to the local time.

10.

Though you may take a midmorning nap, if you feel you need one, avoid the tendency to sleep in the afternoon on your second day at your destination. Instead, walk in bright light or sit near a bright light and glance at it every few minutes between 1 and 4 P.M. NOTE: Do not look directly at the sun or a halogen bulb.

11.

SECOND EVENING AT DESTINATION: If possible, you should go to bed by 6 P.M. Before going to bed, put on a cloth eyemask. Have your dark glasses available so that you can put them on in place of the mask should you have to get out of bed in the middle of the night. NOTE: Don't wear the dark glasses if the light level is too low for them to be worn safely.

12.

SECOND NIGHT AT DESTINATION: If you must arise from bed for any reason between 6 P.M. and 2 A.M., be sure that you replace your eyemask with the dark glasses. Avoiding bright light before 2 A.M. will help you avoid jet lag. Always be careful as you walk with the glasses on. NOTE: Don't wear the dark glasses if the light level is too low for them to be worn safely. Though you will be likely to awaken early, resist the tendency to arise before 2 A.M. If you can stay in bed later, try doing so.

13.

THIRD EVENING AT DESTINATION: Your flight has been a difficult one. If you feel as though you have not fully adjusted to local time by your third day at your destination, you may need an optional booster of light exposure. Sit near a bright light and glance at it every few minutes between 4 and 6 P.M. NOTE: Do not look directly at the sun or a halogen bulb. This last round of light exposure will help lock your body clock in to the desired time zone. You will have accomplished in less than three days what would normally take your body a week and a half!

Table of Cities

1. Look at the column on the left side of the grid and find the city that is your point of departure. If your departure city is not listed, find a nearby city that you believe lies in the same time zone.

2. Look at the row at the top of the grid and find the city that is your destination. If your destination city is not listed, find a nearby city that you believe lies in the same time zone.

3. Find the box where the row naming your departure city and the column naming your destination city meet. In that box you will find the number of time zones you will be crossing and the direction in which you will be traveling. Then, find the instructions for your flight on the pages listed below. (Because the symptoms of jet lag are minimal when one travels through only one or two time zones, we have only included tables for flights that cross three time zones or more.)

If You Are Traveling West to East		*If You Are Traveling East to West*	
Number of Time Zones You Will Cross	*Instructions for Beating Jet Lag on Page*	*Number of Time Zones You Will Cross*	*Instructions for Beating Jet Lag on Page*
3 (Day/Eve. Flight*)	35	3	88
3 (Overnight*)	37	4	91
4	39	5	93
5	41	6	96
6	45	7	99
7	49	8	102
8	54	9	106
9	60	10	111
10	66	11	116
11	73	12	120
12	80	13	125

*The instructions for flying eastward across three time zones differ depending on whether one flies during the day or overnight. Be sure to consult the correct set of instructions.

	Amstdm.	Athens	Auckland	Bangkok	Beijing	Bogotá	Bombay	Boston	Brasília	Bucharest
Amstdm. to		1E	10E	6E	7E	6W	4E	6W	4W	1E
Athens to	1W		9E	5E	6E	7W	3E	7W	5W	0
Auckland to	10W	9W		4W	3W	8E	6W	8E	10E	9W
Bangkok to	6W	5W	4E		1E	12W	2W	12W	10W	5W
Beijing to	7W	6W	3E	1W		11E	3W	11E	11W	6W
Bogotá to	6E	7E	8W	12W	11W		10E	0	2E	7E
Bombay to	4W	3W	6E	2E	3E	10W		10W	8W	3W
Boston to	6E	7E	8W	12W	11W	0	10E		2E	7E
Brasília to	4E	5E	10E	10E	11E	2W	8E	2W		5E
Bucharest to	1W	0	9E	5E	6E	7W	3E	7W	5W	
Budapest to	0	1E	10E	6E	7E	6W	4E	6W	4W	1E
Buen. Air. to	4E	5E	10W	10E	11E	2W	8E	2W	0	5E
Cairo to	1E	0	9E	5E	6E	7W	3E	7W	5W	0
Calgary to	8E	9E	6W	10W	9W	2E	12W	2E	4E	9E
Caracas to	5E	6E	9W	11E	12W	1W	9E	1W	1E	6E
Chicago to	7E	8E	7W	11W	10W	1E	11E	1E	3E	8E
Copenhagen to	0	1E	10E	6E	7E	6W	4E	6W	4W	1E
Dallas to	7E	8E	7W	11W	10W	1E	11E	1E	3E	8E
Denver to	8E	9E	6W	10W	9W	2E	12W	2E	4E	9E
Detroit to	6E	7E	8W	12W	11W	0	10E	0	2E	7E
Frankfurt to	0	1E	10E	6E	7E	6W	4E	6W	4W	1E
Helsinki to	1W	0	9E	5E	6E	7W	3E	7W	5W	0
Hong Kong to	7W	6W	3E	1W	0	11E	3W	11E	11W	6W
Honolulu to	11E	12W	3W	7W	6W	5E	9W	5E	7E	12W
Johanes. to	1W	0	9E	5E	6E	7W	3E	7W	5W	0
Kuwait City to	2W	1W	8E	4E	5E	8W	2E	8W	6W	1W
Lima to	6E	7E	8W	12W	11W	0	10E	0	2E	7E
Lisbon to	1E	2E	11E	7E	8E	5W	5E	5W	3W	2E
London to	1E	2E	11E	7E	8E	5W	5E	5W	3W	2E
Los Angl. to	9E	10E	5W	9W	8W	3E	11W	3E	5E	10E
Madrid to	0	1E	10E	6E	7E	6W	4E	6W	4W	1E
Manila to	7W	6W	3E	1W	0	11E	3W	11E	11W	6W
Mex. City to	7E	8E	7W	11W	10W	1E	11E	1E	3E	8E
Miami to	6E	7E	8W	12W	11W	0	10E	0	2E	7E
Montreal to	6E	7E	8W	12W	11W	0	10E	0	2E	7E
Moscow to	2W	1W	8E	4E	5E	8W	2E	8W	6W	1W
Munich to	0	1E	10E	6E	7E	6W	4E	6W	4W	1E
Nairobi to	2W	1W	8E	4E	5E	8W	2E	8W	6W	1W
New Delhi to	4W	3W	6E	2E	3E	10W	0	10W	8W	3W
New York to	6E	7E	8W	12W	11W	0	10E	0	2E	7E
Paris to	0	1E	10E	6E	7E	6W	4E	6W	4W	1E
Prague to	0	1E	10E	6E	7E	6W	4E	6W	4W	1E
Rio. d. Jan. to	4E	5E	10W	10E	11E	2W	8E	2W	0	5E
Riyadh to	2W	1W	8E	4E	5E	8W	2E	8W	6W	1W
Rome to	0	1E	10E	6E	7E	6W	4E	6W	4W	1E
San Juan to	5E	6E	9W	11E	12W	1W	9E	1W	1E	6E
Seoul to	8W	7W	2E	2W	1W	10E	4W	10E	12W	7W
Singapore to	6W	5W	4E	0	1E	12W	2W	12W	10W	5W
St. Ptburg to	2W	1W	8E	4E	5E	8W	2E	8W	6W	1W
Stockholm to	0	1E	10E	6E	7E	6W	4E	6W	4W	1E
Sydney to	9W	8W	1E	3W	2W	9E	5W	9E	11E	8W
Taipei to	8W	7W	2E	2W	1W	10E	4W	10E	12W	7W
Tel Aviv to	1W	0	9E	5E	6E	7W	3E	7W	5W	0
Tokyo to	8W	7W	2E	2W	1W	10E	4W	10E	12W	7W
Toronto to	6E	7E	8W	12W	11W	0	10E	0	2E	7E
Vancouver to	9E	10E	5W	9W	8W	3E	11W	3E	5E	10E
Vienna to	0	1E	10E	6E	7E	6W	4E	6W	4W	1E
Warsaw to	0	1E	10E	6E	7E	6W	4E	6W	4W	1E
Wash., D.C. to	6E	7E	8W	12W	11W	0	10E	0	2E	7E
Zurich to	0	1E	10E	6E	7E	6W	4E	6W	4W	1E

	Budapest	Buen. Air	Cairo	Calgary	Caracas	Chicago	Copen.	Dallas	Denver	Detroit
Amstdm. to	0	4W	1E	8W	5W	7W	0	7W	8W	6W
Athens to	1W	5W	0	9W	6W	8W	1W	8W	9W	7W
Auckland to	10W	10E	9W	6E	9E	7E	10W	7E	6E	8E
Bangkok to	6W	10W	5W	10E	11W	11E	6W	11E	10E	12W
Beijing to	7W	11W	6W	9E	12W	10E	7W	10E	9E	11E
Bogotá to	6E	2E	7E	2W	1E	1W	6E	1W	2W	0
Bombay to	4W	8W	3W	12W	9W	11W	4W	11W	12W	10W
Boston to	6E	2E	7E	2W	1E	1W	6E	1W	2W	0
Brasília to	4E	0	5E	4W	1W	3W	4E	3W	4W	2W
Bucharest to	1W	5W	0	9W	6W	8W	1W	8W	9W	7W
Budapest to		4W	1E	8W	5W	7W	0	7W	8W	6W
Buen. Air. to	4E		5E	4W	1W	3W	4E	3W	4W	2W
Cairo to	1E	5W		9W	6W	8W	1E	8W	9W	7W
Calgary to	8E	4E	9E		3E	1E	8E	1E	0	2E
Caracas to	5E	1E	6E	3W		2W	5E	2W	3W	1W
Chicago to	7E	3E	8E	1W	2E		7E	0	1W	1E
Copenhagen to	0	4W	1E	8W	5W	7W		7W	8W	6W
Dallas to	7E	3E	8E	1W	2E	0	7E		1W	1E
Denver to	8E	4E	9E	0	3E	1E	8E	1E		2E
Detroit to	6E	2E	7E	2W	1E	1W	6E	1W	2W	
Frankfurt to	0	4W	1E	8W	5W	7W	0	7W	8W	6W
Helsinki to	1W	5W	0	9W	6W	8W	1W	8W	9W	7W
Hong Kong to	7W	11W	6W	9E	12W	10E	7W	10E	9E	11E
Honolulu to	11E	7E	12W	3E	6E	4E	11E	4E	3E	5E
Johanes. to	1W	5W	0	9W	6W	8W	1W	8W	9W	7W
Kuwait City to	2W	6W	1W	10W	7W	9W	2W	9W	10W	8W
Lima to	6E	2E	7E	2W	1E	1W	6E	1W	2W	0
Lisbon to	1E	3W	2E	7W	4W	6W	1E	6W	7W	5W
London to	1E	3W	2E	7W	4W	6W	1E	6W	7W	5W
Los Angl. to	9E	5E	10E	1E	4E	2E	9E	2E	1E	3E
Madrid to	0	4W	1E	8W	5W	7W	0	7W	8W	6W
Manila to	7W	11W	6W	9E	12W	10E	7W	10E	9E	11E
Mex. City to	7E	3E	8E	1W	2E	0	7E	0	1W	1E
Miami to	6E	2E	7E	2W	1E	1W	6E	1W	2W	0
Montreal to	6E	2E	7E	2W	1E	1W	6E	1W	2W	0
Moscow to	2W	6W	1W	10W	7W	9W	2W	9W	10W	8W
Munich to	0	4W	1E	8W	5W	7W	0	7W	8W	6W
Nairobi to	2W	6W	1W	10W	7W	9W	2W	9W	10W	8W
New Delhi to	4W	8W	3W	12W	9W	11W	4W	11W	12W	10W
New York to	6E	2E	7E	2W	1E	1W	6E	1W	2W	0
Paris to	0	4W	1E	8W	5W	7W	0	7W	8W	6W
Prague to	0	4W	1E	8W	5W	7W	0	7W	8W	6W
Rio. d. Jan. to	4E	0	5E	4W	1W	3W	4E	3W	4W	2W
Riyadh to	2W	6W	1W	10W	7W	9W	2W	9W	10W	8W
Rome to	0	4W	1E	8W	5W	7W	0	7W	8W	6W
San Juan to	5E	1E	6E	3W	0	2W	5E	2W	3W	1W
Seoul to	8W	12W	7W	8E	11E	9E	8W	9E	8E	10E
Singapore to	6W	10W	5W	10E	11W	11E	6W	11E	10E	12W
St. Ptburg to	2W	6W	1W	10W	7W	9W	2W	9W	10W	8W
Stockholm to	0	4W	1E	8W	5W	7W	0	7W	8W	6W
Sydney to	9W	11E	8W	7E	10E	8E	9W	8E	7E	9E
Taipei to	8W	12W	7W	8E	11E	9E	8W	9E	8E	10E
Tel Aviv to	1W	5W	0	9W	6W	8W	1W	8W	9W	7W
Tokyo to	8W	12W	7W	8E	11E	9E	8W	9E	8E	10E
Toronto to	6E	2E	7E	2W	1E	1W	6E	1W	2W	0
Vancouver to	9E	5E	10E	1E	4E	2E	9E	2E	1E	3E
Vienna to	0	4W	1E	8W	5W	7W	0	7W	8W	6W
Warsaw to	0	4W	1E	8W	5W	7W	0	7W	8W	6W
Wash., D.C. to	6E	2E	7E	2W	1E	1W	6E	1W	2W	0
Zurich to	0	4W	1E	8W	5W	7W	0	7W	8W	6W

	Frankfurt	Helsinki	Hng Kng	Honolulu	Johanes.	Kuwait	Lima	Lisbon	London	Los Angl.
Amstdm. to	0	1E	7E	11W	1E	2E	6W	1W	1W	9W
Athens to	1W	0	6E	12W	0	1E	7W	2W	2W	10W
Auckland to	10W	9W	3W	3E	9W	8W	8E	11W	11W	5E
Bangkok to	6W	5W	1E	7E	5W	4W	12W	7W	7W	9E
Beijing to	7W	6W	0	6E	6W	5W	11E	8W	8W	8E
Bogotá to	6E	7E	11W	5W	7E	8E	0	5E	5E	3W
Bombay to	4W	3W	3E	9E	3W	2W	10W	5W	5W	11E
Boston to	6E	7E	11W	5W	7E	8E	0	5E	5E	3W
Brasília to	4E	5E	11E	7W	5E	6E	2W	3E	3E	5W
Bucharest to	1W	0	6E	12W	0	1E	7W	2W	2W	10W
Budapest to	0	1E	7E	11W	1E	2E	6W	1W	1W	9W
Buen. Air. to	4E	5E	11E	7W	5E	6E	2W	3E	3E	5W
Cairo to	1E	0	6E	12W	0	1E	7W	2W	2W	10W
Calgary to	8E	9E	9W	3W	9E	10E	2E	7E	7E	1
Caracas to	5E	6E	12W	6W	6E	7E	1W	4E	4E	4W
Chicago to	7E	8E	10W	4W	8E	9E	1E	6E	6E	2W
Copenhagen to	0	1E	7E	11W	1E	2E	6W	1W	1W	9W
Dallas to	7E	8E	10W	4W	8E	9E	1E	6E	6E	2W
Denver to	8E	9E	9W	3W	9E	10E	2E	7E	7E	1
Detroit to	6E	7E	11W	5W	7E	8E	0	5E	5E	3W
Frankfurt to		1E	7E	11W	1E	2E	6W	1W	1W	9W
Helsinki to	1W		6E	12W	0	1E	7W	2W	2W	10W
Hong Kong to	7W	6W		6E	6W	5W	11E	8W	8W	8E
Honolulu to	11E	12W	6W		12W	11W	5E	10E	10E	2E
Johanes. to	1W	0	6E	12W		1E	7W	2W	2W	10W
Kuwait City to	2W	1W	5E	11E	1W		8W	3W	3W	11W
Lima to	6E	7E	11W	5W	7E	8E		5E	5E	3W
Lisbon to	1E	2E	8E	10W	2E	3E	5W		0	8W
London to	1E	2E	8E	10W	2E	3E	5W	0		8W
Los Angl. to	9E	10E	8W	2W	10E	11E	3E	8E	8E	
Madrid to	0	1E	7E	11W	1E	2E	6W	1W	1W	9W
Manila to	7W	6W	0	6E	6W	5W	11E	8W	8W	8E
Mex. City to	7E	8E	10W	4W	8E	9E	1E	6E	6E	2W
Miami to	6E	7E	11W	5W	7E	8E	0	5E	5E	3W
Montreal to	6E	7E	11W	5W	7E	8E	0	5E	5E	3W
Moscow to	2W	1W	5E	11E	1W	0	8W	3W	3W	11W
Munich to	0	1E	7E	11W	1E	2E	6W	1W	1W	9W
Nairobi to	2W	1W	5E	11E	1W	0	8W	3W	3W	11W
New Delhi to	4W	3W	3E	9E	3W	2W	10W	5W	5W	11E
New York to	6E	7E	11W	5W	7E	8E	0	5E	5E	3W
Paris to	0	1E	7E	11W	1E	2E	6W	1W	1W	9W
Prague to	0	1E	7E	11W	1E	2E	6W	1W	1W	9W
Rio. d. Jan. to	4E	5E	11E	7W	5E	6E	2W	3E	3E	5W
Riyadh to	2W	1W	5E	11E	1W	0	8W	3W	3W	11W
Rome to	0	1E	7E	11W	1E	2E	6W	1W	1W	9W
San Juan to	5E	6E	12W	6W	6E	7E	1W	4E	4E	4W
Seoul to	8W	7W	1W	5E	7W	6W	10E	9W	9W	7E
Singapore to	6W	5W	1E	7E	5W	4W	12W	7W	7W	9E
St. Ptburg to	2W	1W	5E	11E	1W	0	8W	3W	3W	11W
Stockholm to	0	1E	7E	11W	1E	2E	6W	1W	1W	9W
Sydney to	9W	8W	2W	4E	8W	7W	9E	10W	10W	6E
Taipei to	8W	7W	1W	5E	7W	6W	10E	9W	9W	7E
Tel Aviv to	1W	0	6E	12W	0	1E	7W	2W	2W	10W
Tokyo to	8W	7W	1W	5E	7W	6W	10E	9W	9W	7E
Toronto to	6E	7E	11W	5W	7E	8E	0	5E	5E	3W
Vancouver to	9E	10E	8W	2W	10E	11E	3E	8E	8E	0
Vienna to	0	1E	7E	11W	1E	2E	6W	1W	1W	9W
Warsaw to	0	1E	7E	11W	1E	2E	6W	1W	1W	9W
Wash., D.C. to	6E	7E	11W	5W	7E	8E	0	5E	5E	3W
Zurich to	0	1E	7E	11W	1E	2E	6W	1W	1W	9W

	Madrid	Manila	Mex. City	Miami	Montreal	Moscow	Munich	Nairobi	N. Delhi	New York
Amstdm. to	0	7E	7W	6W	6W	2E	0	2E	4E	6W
Athens to	1W	6E	8W	7W	7W	1E	1W	1E	3E	7W
Auckland to	10W	3W	7E	8E	8E	8W	10W	8W	6W	8E
Bangkok to	6W	1E	11E	12W	12W	4W	6W	4W	2W	12W
Beijing to	7W	0	10E	11E	11E	5W	7W	5W	3W	11E
Bogotá to	6E	11W	1W	0	0	8E	6E	8E	10E	0
Bombay to	4W	3E	11W	10W	10W	2W	4W	2W	0	10W
Boston to	6E	11W	1W	0	0	8E	6E	8E	10E	0
Brasília to	4E	11E	3W	2W	2W	6E	4E	6E	8E	2W
Bucharest to	1W	6E	8W	7W	7W	1E	1W	1E	3E	7W
Budapest to	0	7E	7W	6W	6W	2E	0	2E	4E	6W
Buen. Air. to	4E	11E	3W	2W	2W	6E	4E	6E	8E	2W
Cairo to	1E	6E	8W	7W	7W	1E	1E	1E	3E	7W
Calgary to	8E	9W	1E	2E	2E	10E	8E	10E	12W	2E
Caracas to	5E	12W	2W	1W	1W	7E	5E	7E	9E	1W
Chicago to	7E	10W	0	1E	1E	9E	7E	9E	11E	1E
Copenhagen to	0	7E	7W	6W	6W	2E	0	2E	4E	6W
Dallas to	7E	10W	0	1E	1E	9E	7E	9E	11E	1E
Denver to	8E	9W	1E	2E	2E	10E	8E	10E	12W	2E
Detroit to	6E	11W	1W	0	0	8E	6E	8E	10E	0
Frankfurt to	0	7E	7W	6W	6W	2E	0	2E	4E	6W
Helsinki to	1W	6E	8W	7W	7W	1E	1W	1E	3E	7W
Hong Kong to	7W	0	10E	11E	11E	5W	7W	5W	3W	11E
Honolulu to	11E	6W	4E	5E	5E	11W	11E	11W	9W	5E
Johanes. to	1W	6E	8W	7W	7W	1E	1W	1E	3E	7W
Kuwait City to	2W	5E	9W	8W	8W	0	2W	0	2E	8W
Lima to	6E	11W	1W	0	0	8E	6E	8E	10E	0
Lisbon to	1E	8E	6W	5W	5W	3E	1E	3E	5E	5W
London to	1E	8E	6W	5W	5W	3E	1E	3E	5E	5W
Los Angl. to	9E	8W	2E	3E	3E	11E	9E	11E	11W	3E
Madrid to		7E	7W	6W	6W	2E	0	2E	4E	6W
Manila to	7W		10E	11E	11E	5W	7W	5W	3W	11E
Mex. City to	7E	10W		1E	1E	9E	7E	9E	11E	1E
Miami to	6E	11W	1W		0	8E	6E	8E	10E	0
Montreal to	6E	11W	1W	0		8E	6E	8E	10E	0
Moscow to	2W	5E	9W	8W	8W		2W	0	2E	8W
Munich to	0	7E	7W	6W	6W	2E		2E	4E	6W
Nairobi to	2W	5E	9W	8W	8W	0	2W		2E	8W
New Delhi to	4W	3E	11W	10W	10W	2W	4W	2W		10W
New York to	6E	11W	1W	0	0	8E	6E	8E	10E	
Paris to	0	7E	7W	6W	6W	2E	0	2E	4E	6W
Prague to	0	7E	7W	6W	6W	2E	0	2E	4E	6W
Rio. d. Jan. to	4E	11E	3W	2W	2W	6E	4E	6E	8E	2W
Riyadh to	2W	5E	9W	8W	8W	0	2W	0	2E	8W
Rome to	0	7E	7W	6W	6W	2E	0	2E	4E	6W
San Juan to	5E	12W	2W	1W	1W	7E	5E	7E	9E	1W
Seoul to	8W	1W	9E	10E	10E	6W	8W	6W	4W	10E
Singapore to	6W	1E	11E	12W	12W	4W	6W	4W	2W	12W
St. Ptburg to	2W	5E	9W	8W	8W	0	2W	0	2E	8W
Stockholm to	0	7E	7W	6W	6W	2E	0	2E	4E	6W
Sydney to	9W	2W	8E	9E	9E	7W	9W	7W	5W	9E
Taipei to	8W	1W	9E	10E	10E	6W	8W	6W	4W	10E
Tel Aviv to	1W	6E	8W	7W	7W	1E	1W	1E	3E	7W
Tokyo to	8W	1W	9E	10E	10E	6W	8W	6W	4W	10E
Toronto to	6E	11W	1W	0	0	8E	6E	8E	10E	0
Vancouver to	9E	8W	2E	3E	3E	11E	9E	11E	11W	3E
Vienna to	0	7E	7W	6W	6W	2E	0	2E	4E	6W
Warsaw to	0	7E	7W	6W	6W	2E	0	2E	4E	6W
Wash., D.C. to	6E	11W	1W	0	0	8E	6E	8E	10E	0
Zurich to	0	7E	7W	6W	6W	2E	0	2E	4E	6W

	Paris	Prague	Rio d.Jan.	Riyadh	Rome	San Juan	Seoul	Singpor.	St. Ptburg	Stockhm.
Amstdm. to	0	0	4W	2E	0	5W	8E	6E	2E	0
Athens to	1W	1W	5W	1E	1W	6W	7E	5E	1E	1E
Auckland to	10W	10W	10E	8W	10W	9E	2W	4W	8W	10W
Bangkok to	6W	6W	10W	4W	6W	11W	2E	0	4W	6W
Beijing to	7W	7W	11W	5W	7W	12W	1E	1W	5W	7W
Bogotá to	6E	6E	2E	8E	6E	1E	10W	12W	8E	6E
Bombay to	4W	4W	8W	2W	4W	9W	4E	2E	2W	4W
Boston to	6E	6E	2E	8E	6E	1E	10W	12W	8E	6E
Brasília to	4E	4E	0	6E	4E	1W	12W	10E	6E	4E
Bucharest to	1W	1W	5W	1E	1W	6W	7E	5E	1E	1E
Budapest to	0	0	4W	2E	0	5W	8E	6E	2E	0
Buen. Air. to	4E	4E	0	6E	4E	1W	12W	10E	6E	4E
Cairo to	1E	1E	5W	1E	1E	6W	7E	5E	1E	1E
Calgary to	8E	8E	4E	10E	8E	3E	8W	10W	10E	8E
Caracas to	5E	5E	1E	7E	5E	0	11W	11E	7E	5E
Chicago to	7E	7E	3E	9E	7E	2E	9W	11W	9E	7E
Copenhagen to	0	0	4W	2E	0	5W	8E	6E	2E	0
Dallas to	7E	7E	3E	9E	7E	2E	9W	11W	9E	7E
Denver to	8E	8E	4E	10E	8E	3E	8W	10W	10E	8E
Detroit to	6E	6E	2E	8E	6E	1E	10W	12W	8E	6E
Frankfurt to	0	0	4W	2E	0	5W	8E	6E	2E	0
Helsinki to	1W	1W	5W	1E	1W	6W	7E	5E	1E	1E
Hong Kong to	7W	7W	11W	5W	7W	12W	1E	1W	5W	7W
Honolulu to	11E	11E	7E	11W	11E	6E	5W	7W	11W	11E
Johanes. to	1W	1W	5W	1E	1W	6W	7E	5E	1E	1E
Kuwait City to	2W	2W	6W	0	2W	7W	6E	4E	0	2W
Lima to	6E	6E	2E	8E	6E	1E	10W	12W	8E	6E
Lisbon to	1E	1E	3W	3E	1E	4W	9E	7E	3E	1E
London to	1E	1E	3W	3E	1E	4W	9E	7E	3E	1E
Los Angl. to	9E	9E	5E	11E	9E	4E	7W	9W	11E	9E
Madrid to	0	0	4W	2E	0	5W	8E	6E	2E	0
Manila to	7W	7W	11W	5W	7W	12W	1E	1W	5W	7W
Mex. City to	7E	7E	3E	9E	7E	2E	9W	11W	9E	7E
Miami to	6E	6E	2E	8E	6E	1E	10W	12W	8E	6E
Montreal to	6E	6E	2E	8E	6E	1E	10W	12W	8E	6E
Moscow to	2W	2W	6W	0	2W	7W	6E	4E	0	2W
Munich to	0	0	4W	2E	0	5W	8E	6E	2E	0
Nairobi to	2W	2W	6W	0	2W	7W	6E	4E	0	2W
New Delhi to	4W	4W	8W	2W	4W	9W	4E	2E	2W	4W
New York to	6E	6E	2E	8E	6E	1E	10W	12W	8E	6E
Paris to		0	4W	2E	0	5W	8E	6E	2E	0
Prague to	0		4W	2E	0	5W	8E	6E	2E	0
Rio. d. Jan. to	4E	4E		6E	4E	1W	12W	10E	6E	4E
Riyadh to	2W	2W	6W		2W	7W	6E	4E	0	2W
Rome to	0	0	4W	2E		5W	8E	6E	2E	0
San Juan to	5E	5E	1E	7E	5E		11W	11E	7E	5E
Seoul to	8W	8W	12W	6W	8W	11E		2W	6W	8W
Singapore to	6W	6W	10W	4W	6W	11W	2E		4W	6W
St. Ptburg to	2W	2W	6W	0	2W	7W	6E	4E		2W
Stockholm to	0	0	4W	2E	0	5W	8E	6E	2E	
Sydney to	9W	9W	11E	7W	9W	10E	1W	3W	7W	9W
Taipei to	8W	8W	12W	6W	8W	11E	0	2W	6W	8W
Tel Aviv to	1W	1W	5W	1E	1W	6W	7E	5E	1E	1E
Tokyo to	8W	8W	12W	6W	8W	11E	0	2W	6W	8W
Toronto to	6E	6E	2E	8E	6E	1E	10W	12W	8E	6E
Vancouver to	9E	9E	5E	11E	9E	4E	7W	9W	11E	9E
Vienna to	0	0	4W	2E	0	5W	8E	6E	2E	0
Warsaw to	0	0	4W	2E	0	5W	8E	6E	2E	0
Wash., D.C. to	6E	6E	2E	8E	6E	1E	10W	12W	8E	6E
Zurich to	0	0	4W	2E	0	5W	8E	6E	2E	0

	Sydney	Taipei	Tel Aviv	Tokyo	Toronto	Vancouv.	Vienna	Warsaw	Wash D.C.	Zurich
Amstdm. to	9E	8E	1E	8E	6W	9W	0	0	6	0
Athens to	8E	7E	0	7E	7W	10W	1W	1W	7W	1W
Auckland to	1W	2W	9W	2W	8E	5E	10W	10W	8E	10W
Bangkok to	3E	2E	5W	2E	12W	9E	6W	6W	12W	6W
Beijing to	2E	1E	6W	1E	11E	8E	7W	7W	11E	7W
Bogotá to	9W	10W	7E	10W	0	3W	6E	6E	0	6E
Bombay to	5E	4E	3W	4E	10W	11E	4W	4W	10W	4W
Boston to	9W	10W	7E	10W	0	3W	6E	6E	0	6E
Brasília to	11W	12W	5E	12W	2W	5W	4E	4E	2W	4E
Bucharest to	8E	7E	0	7E	7W	10W	1W	1W	7W	1W
Budapest to	9E	8E	1E	8E	6W	9W	0	0	6W	0
Buen. Air. to	11W	12W	5E	12W	2W	5W	4E	4E	2W	4E
Cairo to	8E	7E	0	7E	7W	10W	1E	1E	7W	1E
Calgary to	7W	8W	9E	8W	2E	1	8E	8E	2E	8E
Caracas to	10W	11W	6E	11W	1W	4W	5E	5E	1W	5E
Chicago to	8W	9W	8E	9W	1E	2W	7E	7E	1E	7E
Copenhagen to	9E	8E	1E	8E	6W	9W	0	0	6W	0
Dallas to	8W	9W	8E	9W	1E	2W	7E	7E	1E	7E
Denver to	7W	8W	9E	8W	2E	1	8E	8E	2E	8E
Detroit to	9W	10W	7E	10W	0	3W	6E	6E	0	6E
Frankfurt to	9E	8E	1E	8E	6W	9W	0	0	6W	0
Helsinki to	8E	7E	0	7E	7W	10W	1W	1W	7W	1W
Hong Kong to	2E	1E	6W	1E	11E	8E	7W	7W	11E	7W
Honolulu to	4W	5W	12W	5W	5E	2E	11E	11E	5E	11E
Johanes. to	8E	7E	0	7E	7W	10W	1W	1W	7W	1W
Kuwait City to	7E	6E	1W	6E	8W	11W	2W	2W	8W	2W
Lima to	9W	10W	7E	10W	0	3W	6E	6E	0	6E
Lisbon to	10E	9E	2E	9E	5W	8W	1E	1E	5W	1E
London to	10E	9E	2E	9E	5W	8W	1E	1E	5W	1E
Los Angl. to	6W	7W	10E	7W	3E	0	9E	9E	3E	9E
Madrid to	9E	8E	1E	8E	6W	9W	0	0	6W	0
Manila to	2E	1E	6W	1E	11E	8E	7W	7W	11E	7W
Mex. City to	8W	9W	8E	9W	1E	2W	7E	7E	1E	7E
Miami to	9W	10W	7E	10W	0	3W	6E	6E	0	6E
Montreal to	9W	10W	7E	10W	0	3W	6E	6E	0	6E
Moscow to	7E	6E	1W	6E	8W	11W	2W	2W	8W	2W
Munich to	9E	8E	1E	8E	6W	9W	0	0	6W	0
Nairobi to	7E	6E	1W	6E	8W	11W	2W	2W	8W	2W
New Delhi to	5E	4E	3W	4E	10W	11E	4W	4W	10W	4W
New York to	9W	10W	7E	10W	0	3W	6E	6E	0	6E
Paris to	9E	8E	1E	8E	6W	9W	0	0	6W	0
Prague to	9E	8E	1E	8E	6W	9W	0	0	6W	0
Rio. d. Jan. to	11W	12W	5E	12W	2W	5W	4E	4E	2W	4E
Riyadh to	7E	6E	1W	6E	8W	11W	2W	2W	8W	2W
Rome to	9E	8E	1E	8E	6W	9W	0	0	6W	0
San Juan to	10W	11W	6E	11W	1W	4W	5E	5E	1W	5E
Seoul to	1E	0	7W	0	10E	7E	8W	8W	10E	8W
Singapore to	3E	2E	5W	2E	12W	9E	6W	6W	12W	6W
St. Ptburg to	7E	6E	1W	6E	8W	11W	2W	2W	8W	2W
Stockholm to	9E	8E	1E	8E	6W	9W	0	0	6W	0
Sydney to		1W	8W	1W	9E	6E	9W	9W	9E	9W
Taipei to	1E		7W	0	10E	7E	8W	8W	10E	8W
Tel Aviv to	8E	7E		7E	7W	10W	1W	1W	7W	1W
Tokyo to	1E	0	7W		10E	7E	8W	8W	10E	8W
Toronto to	9W	10W	7E	10W		3W	6E	6E	0	6E
Vancouver to	6W	7W	10E	7W	3E		9E	9E	3E	9E
Vienna to	9E	8E	1E	8E	6W	9W		0	6W	0
Warsaw to	9E	8E	1E	8E	6W	9W	0		6W	0
"Wash., D.C. to"	9W	10W	7E	10W	0	3W	6E	6E		6E
Zurich to	9E	8E	1E	8E	6W	9W	0	0	6W	